poetry

WINTER SONG

WINTER SONG

An Anthology of Poems
on Old Age

EDITED BY

Georgina Battiscombe

CONSTABLE · LONDON

First published in Great Britain 1992
by Constable & Company Limited
3 The Lanchesters, 162 Fulham Palace Road
London W6 9ER
Copyright arrangement and editorial matter
© 1992 by Georgina Battiscombe
The right of Georgina Battiscombe to be
identified as the author of this work
has been asserted by her in accordance
with the Copyright, Designs and Patents Act 1988
For copyright holders of poems, see Acknowledgements
ISBN 0 09 470990 4
Set in Monophoto Apollo by
Servis Filmsetting Limited, Manchester
Printed in Great Britain by
St Edmundsbury Press Limited
Bury St Edmunds, Suffolk

A CIP catalogue record for this book
is available from the British Library

IN MEMORIAM CFB

Contents

BEAUTY VANISHES, BEAUTY PASSES

HUSBAND AND WIFE

CONTENTS

9

PAINS AND INDIGNITIES

COMFORT AND JOY

CONTENTS

LOOKING BACKWARD

LOOKING FORWARD

CONTENTS

EPILOGUE

Acknowledgements

My grateful thanks are due to the many people who have helped me with this anthology, in particular to Guy Andrews, Elizabeth Brunner, Margaret Elphinstone, Ruth Harris, Alethea Hayter, George Harwood, Margaret Hill, David Hopkinson, Mary Wedd, and most especially to Margaret Valk and Elizabeth Willis.

The publishers and Georgina Battiscombe would like to thank the following for their kind permission to quote the following poems which are in copyright: Messrs Faber & Bafer for W.H. Auden's 'Old People's Home', T.S. Eliot's 'A Song for Simeon', and Philip Larkin's 'The Winter Palace', 'Age', 'Heads in the Women's Ward', 'The Old Fools', 'Continuing to Live' and 'Long Sight in Age'; the late George Barker for 'To my Mother'; Messrs John Murray for John Betjeman's 'Late-flowering Lust' and 'Felixstowe, or The Last of Her Order'; Carcanet Press for Edmund Blunden's 'Almswomen', and Iain Crighton Smith's 'Old Woman'; Guy Butler for his 'Great-great-grandmother'; Simon Campbell for Joseph Campbell's 'The Old Woman'; MBA Literary Agents for Catherine Carswell's 'Envoy'; the Estate of Katherine Chorley for 'The Hearth'; The Estate of Frances Cornford and The Cresset Press for 'All Soul's Night', 'Childhood' and 'Old Men outside an Inn'; the Rev. Stephen Hopkinson for Margaret Cropper's 'Growing Old', 'Old Age' and 'I'll hold your Hand'; Peters Fraser & Dunlop for the extract from C. Day Lewis's 'My Mother's Sister'; Macmillan for Colin Ellis's 'The Old Ladies', and for R.S. Thomas's 'The Country Clergy' and 'Seventieth Birthday'; The Estate of William Empson and The Hogarth Press for 'To an Old Lady'; Watson Little for D.J. Enright's 'Geriatrics'; the Estate of Oliver Gogarty for 'Non Dolet'; F. Pratt Green for 'The Old Couple'; Diana Hendry for 'Prayer for Rain'; David Higham Associates for Elizabeth Jennings' 'Old Man', 'Old Woman', 'One Flesh' and 'Rembrandt's Later Self Portraits', for Edith Sitwell's 'An Old Woman Laments in Spring-time', David Higham Associates and Weidenfeld/Dent for Dylan Thomas's 'Do not go gentle into that good night' and 'Youth Calls to Age'; John Johnson for Jenny Joseph's 'Warning' and 'Trompe l'oeil'; The Society of Authors for Walter de la Mare's 'All gone', 'Age', 'Old Ben', 'Alone', 'Dust to Dust' and 'The Old Man', and for John Masefield's 'On Growing Old'; Henry Markham for 'Old Age'; the Penguin Group (Hamish Hamilton) for Kathleen Raine's 'A Nice Little World' and 'Christmas Tree'; Dr A.L. Rowse for 'The White Cat of Trenarren'; Alison Young for Andrew Young's 'The Old Man' and 'The Blind Man', David Hopkinson for 'Friends of Old Age' and finally Margaret Walker for 'Lineage'.

Introduction

'Age I do abhor thee; Youth, I do adore thee;' such were the sentiments of the majority of English poets up to the time of Wordsworth. Love was their favourite theme, and love and age do not make good bed-fellows. Maybe too they were influenced by the fact that although in the sixteenth and seventeenth centuries old age began as early as sixty no one could, with any real confidence, look forward to reaching that age. Primitive medical practice, lack of the most elementary health measures, frequent wars and rebellions, brawls and duelling, put everyone at risk; in the words of the Prayer Book, 'plague, pestilence and famine, battle, murder and sudden death' were commonplace features of life, as fatal to the young as to the old. Philip Sidney fell in battle at the age of thirty-two, young Christopher Marlowe was killed in a drunken brawl, Walter Raleigh, who wrote some of the most lovely of all poems about death but none about old age, died on the scaffold in his early fifties, accused of fomenting rebellion against James I. Few poets lived to be old men; Shakespeare died aged fifty-two, Spenser forty-seven, Richard Crashaw thirty-six, George Herbert forty, Traherne thirty-seven. George Peele described himself as 'an aged man'. His dates are uncertain; but he was probably no more than forty when he died. It might be worth noting that Herrick, Vaughan, and Waller, three of the very few poets of this period to write about old age, all survived into their seventies.

Precarious though it was, life in the eighteenth century was less 'nasty, brutish and short' than it had been in earlier days. Old age, however, was not a subject to appeal to the poets of the Age of Elegance. If they wrote of it at all it was to stress its serene, benevolent aspect. Old people, as eighteenth century poets portray them, 'Sink to the grave with unperceived decay While resignation gently slopes the way.' Writing of an eighty-year-old Doctor Johnson assures us that 'His frame was firm, his powers were bright'; no talk here of mental decline, loss of memory or the inevitable squalor of physical decrepitude.

It was for Wordsworth, a so-called 'Romantic' poet, to look old age squarely in the face and to see it as a proper subject for great poetry. (He

15

himself lived to be eighty.) Since his intention was 'to choose incidents and situations from common life and to describe them in a selection of language really used by men' it is not surprising that he should write much about the old people whom he saw around him in the Cumbrian dales. He does not stress the ugliness of old age but neither does he see it as a happy period. He knows it to be a time when mind and body inevitably decay but when soul and spirit can, and often do, soar and take wing. The best of Wordsworth's poems on old age, as, for instance, the Matthew poems (see page 41) were written when he himself was a young man. He looks at old age from the outside, as it were, feeling for the old a deep pity and a certain reverence. His old people are sad but they are also serene; and from them the young can learn wisdom.

The Victorian poets, as a whole, took an optimistic and romantic view of old age although not all of them believed with Browning that the last of life was also the best. The Georgians, and in particular Walter de la Mare, saw much more of its sadness, but they remained in essence romantic rather than realist in their approach.

August 1914 changed the face of the world, and with this change came an alteration in the style and subject-matter of poetry. Wordsworth had been the first poet to use ordinary language to describe the ordinary; the war poets were the first to use ugly language to describe ugliness. They had no option, for they were writing about modern war, which is a very ugly thing, not to be written of in the same language that Tennyson used to describe the charge of the Light Brigade. (That episode cannot in fact have been a very pretty one.) In *King Lear* the blinding of Gloucester is horrible enough, but it is described as a tragic rather than an ugly event. The poets of the 1914–18 War were the first to see sheer ugliness as an acceptable, indeed as an unavoidable subject for poetry.

In the second half of the twentieth century expectancy of life has increased remarkably. The days of our age are no longer three score years and ten, but four score years or more. The average age of the population is continually rising; modern poets see old age all around them and they do not like what they see. Brought up on the poetry of Sassoon, Owen and Rosenberg they do not spare the reader any ugly detail, and some of them, though not all, see the squalor of age rather than its serenity. To paraphrase Wilfred Owen's much-quoted sentence, their subject is age and the pity of age and the poetry inevitably lies in the pity. Two poems by Philip Larkin illustrate this point. *The Old Fools* is a brilliant poem, but it is devoid of pity and therefore the reader feels no sort of catharsis or uplift but merely revulsion. A lesser-known poem, *Women's Ward*, is, to my mind, a better poem because, unflinching though it is in its description of mental and physical decay, it has in it the cleansing element of pity.

Contemporary with but in many ways apart from both the war poets and the moderns are two major poets of old age, W.B. Yeats and T.S. Eliot. Yeats writes from the personal point of view of an old man. Unlike Browning, he sees old age as in itself bad, a ludicrous, ugly joke like a tin-can 'tied to me as to a dog's tail', but in the same poem he writes 'Now shall I make my soul', using, oddly enough, a conventional religious term often applied to the period of old age. The man himself can bring good out of this evil; he can use old age as a time for soul-making and emerge from it a better and more remarkable person than ever he was in the pride of his youth. Given 'an old man's frenzy', he can achieve 'an old man's eagle mind'.

Although, like Yeats, Eliot lived into his seventies, he writes mainly from the outside and as an observer. Unfortunately, copyright restrictions have prevented the inclusion of famous passages from *Four Quartets* and from *The Love Song of J. Alfred Prufrock*. *The Song of Simeon* is, arguably, the greatest modern poem about old age. His longer poem, *Gerontion*, is much more obscure and cannot be abbreviated to fit into an anthology. This question of abbreviation has been a serious problem. In her preface to *The New Oxford Book of English Verse* Dame Helen Gardner argues that it is permissible to take excerpts from long poems and print them as poems in their own right. (Strangely enough, it is not possible to find any suitable excerpt dealing with old age in *King Lear*, Shakespeare's great tragedy on that subject.) Is it equally permissible to cut the long poem itself down to the necessary size and print it in a truncated version?

Michael, perhaps the most notable of Wordsworth's poems on old age, cannot possibly be abbreviated, but fortunately *Resolution and Independence* is more adaptable. Worst of all is the problem of Browning's *Rabbi ben Ezra*, which is far too long to fit into an anthology. I felt that a poem so well-known and well-loved must obviously be included, and therefore I have attempted to cut it, but I cannot say that I am pleased with the result.

This anthology contains much good and some great poetry, maybe also two or three poems which might be classed as bad. They have been included because they illustrate some particular aspect of old age, a period of life which, although we may not live to see it, we must prepare ourselves to enjoy or to endure.

Prologue

W.B. YEATS

1865–1939

From *Sailing to Byzantium*

An aged man is but a paltry thing,
A tattered coat upon a stick, unless
Soul clap its hands, and sing, and louder sing
For every tatter in its mortal dress,
Nor is there singing school but studying
Monuments of its own magnificence;
And therefore have I sailed the seas and come
To the holy city of Byzantium

Anticipation

ROBERT BROWNING

1812–1889

Rabbi Ben Ezra

Grow old along with me!
The best is yet to be,
The last of life for which the first was made:
Our times are in His hand
Who saith, 'A whole I planned,
'Youth shows but half; trust God: see all nor be afraid!' . . .

Therefore I summon age
To grant's youth's heritage,
Life's struggle having so far reached its term:
Thence shall I pass, approved
A man, for aye removed
From the developed brute; a god though in the germ.

And I shall thereupon
Take rest, ere I be gone
Once more on my adventure brave and new:
Fearless and unperplexed,
When I wage battle next,
What weapons to select, what armour to indue.

Youth ended, I shall try
My gain or loss thereby;
Leave the fire ashes, what survives is gold:
And I shall weigh the same,
Give life its praise or blame:
Young, all lay in dispute; I shall know, being old.

For note, when evening shuts,
A certain moment cuts
The deed off, calls the glory from the grey:
A whisper from the west
Shoots – 'Add this to the rest,
'Take it and try its worth : here dies another day'.

So, still within this life
        Though lifted o'er its strife,
    Let me discern, compare, pronounce at last,
        'This rage was right i' the main,
        'That acquiescence vain:
    'The Future I may face now I have proved the Past'. . .

        Not on the vulgar mass
        Called 'work', must sentence pass,
    Things done, that took the eye and had the price;
        O'er which, from level stand
        The low world laid its hand,
    Found straightway to its mind, could value in a trice:

        But all, the world's coarse thumb
        And finger failed to plumb,
    So passed in making up the main account;
        All instincts immature,
        All purposes unsure,
    That weighed not as his work, yet swelled the man's amount:

        Thoughts hardly to be packed
        Into a narrow act,
    Fancies that broke through language and escaped;
        All I could never be,
        All men ignored in me,
    This I was worth to God, whose wheel the pitcher shaped.

        Ay, note that Potter's wheel,
        That metaphor! and feel
    Why time spins fast, why passive lies our clay, —
        Thou, to whom fools propound,
        When the wine makes its round,
    'Since life fleets, all is change; the Past gone, seize to-day!'

        Fool! All that is, at all,
        Lasts ever, past recall;
    Earth changes, but thy soul and God stand sure;
        What entered into thee,
        That was, is, and shall be,
    Time's wheel runs back or stops: Potter and clay endure. . .

So, take and use Thy work:
    Amend what flaws may lurk,
What strain o' the stuff, what warpings past the aim!
    My times he in Thy hand!
    Perfect the cup as planned!
Let age approve of youth, and death complete the same!

CHARLES KINGSLEY

1819–1875

The Old Song

When all the world is young, lad,
    And all the trees are green;
And every goose a swan, lad,
    And every lass a queen;
Then hey for boot and horse, lad,
    And round the world away!
Young blood must have its course, lad,
    And every dog his day.

When all the world is old, lad,
    And all the trees are brown;
And all the sport is stale, lad,
    And all the wheels run down;
Creep home, and take your place there
    The spent and maimed among;
God grant you find one face there
    you loved when all was young!

JENNY JOSEPH

1932–

Warning

When I am an old woman I shall wear purple
With a red hat which doesn't go, and doesn't suit me,

And I shall spend my pension on brandy and summer gloves
And satin sandals, and say we've no money for butter.
I shall sit down on the pavement when I'm tired
and gobble up samples in shops and press alarm bells
And run my stick along the public railings
And make up for the sobriety of my youth.
I shall go out in my slippers in the rain
And pick the flowers in other people's gardens
And learn to spit.

You can wear terrible shirts and grow more fat
And eat three pounds of sausages at a go
Or only bread and pickle for a week
And hoard pens and pencils and beermats and things in boxes.

But now we must have clothes that keep us dry
And pay our rent and not swear in the street
And set a good example for the children.
We will have friends to dinner and read the papers,

But maybe I ought to practise a little now?
So people who know me are not too shocked and surprised
When suddenly I am old and start to wear purple.

RUDYARD KIPLING

1865–1936

The Old Men

This is our lot if we live so long and labour unto the end –
That we outlive the impatient years and the much too patient friend:
And because we know we have breath in our mouth and think we have
thoughts in our head.
We shall assume that we are alive, whereas we are really dead.

We shall not acknowledge that old stars fade or brighter planets arise
(That the sere bush buds or the desert blooms or the ancient well-head
dries).

Or any new compass wherewith new men adventure 'neath new skies.

We shall lift up the ropes that constrained our youth, to bind on our
children's hands;
We shall call to the water below the bridges to return and replenish
our lands;
We shall harness horses (Death's own pale horses) and scholarly plough
the sands.

We shall lie down in the eye of the sun for lack of a light on our way –
We shall rise up when the day is done and chirrup, 'Behold, it is day!'
We shall abide till the battle is won ere we amble into the fray.

We shall peck out and discuss and dissect, and evert and extrude to
our mind,
The flaccid tissues of long-dead issues offensive to God and mankind –
(Precisely like vultures over an ox that the Army has left behind).

We shall make walk preposterous ghosts of the glories we once
created –
Immodestly smearing from muddled palettes amazing pigments
mismated –
And our friends will weep when we ask them with boasts if our
natural force be abated.

The Lamp of our Youth will be utterly out, but we shall subsist on the
smell of it;
And whatever we do, we shall fold our hands and suck our gums and
think well of it.
Yes, we shall be perfectly pleased with our work and that is the
Perfectest Hell of it!

This is our lot if we live so long and listen to those who love us –
That we are shunned by the people about and shamed by the Powers above
us.
Wherefore be free of your harness betimes; but, being free, be assured,
That he who hath not endured to the death, from his birth he hath never
endured.

WILLIAM WORDSWORTH

1770—1850

The Small Celandine

There is a flower, the lesser Celandine,
That shrinks, like many more, from cold and rain;
And, the first moment that the sun may shine,
Bright as the sun himself, 'tis out again!

When hailstones have been falling, swarm on swarm,
Or blasts the green field and the trees distrest,
Oft have I seen it muffled up from harm,
In close self-shelter, like a Thing at rest.

But lately, one rough day, this Flower I passed
And recognised it, though an altered form,
Now standing forth, an offering to the blast,
And buffetted at will by rain and storm.

I stopped, and said with inly-muttered voice,
'It doth not love the shower, nor seek the cold:
This neither is its courage nor its choice,
But its necessity in being old.

'The sunshine may not cheer it, nor the dew;
It cannot help itself in its decay;
Stiff in its members, withered, changed of hue.'
And, in my spleen, I smiled that it was grey.

To be a Prodigal's favourite – then worse truth,
A Miser's Pensioner, – behold our lot!
O Man, that from thy fair and shining youth
Age might but take the things youth needed not!

Wordsworth was thirty-four when he wrote this poem.

G.K. CHESTERTON

1874–1936

To M.E.W.

Words, for alas my trade is words, a barren burst of rhymes,
Rubbed by a hundred rhymesters, battered a thousand times,
Take them, you, that smile on strings, those nobler sounds than mine,
The words that never lie, or brag, or flatter, or malign.

I give a hand to my lady, another to my friend,
To whom you too have a hand; and so before the end
We four may pray, for all the years, whatever suns be set,
The sole two prayers worth praying – to live and not forget.

The pale leaf falls in pallor, but the grean leaf turns to gold;
We that have found it good to be young shall find it good to be old;
Life that bringeth the marriage bell, the cradle and the grave,
Life that is mean to the mean of heart, and only brave to the brave.

In the calm of the last white winter, when all the past is ours,
Old tears are frozen as jewels, old storms frosted as flowers,
Dear Lady, may we meet again, stand up again, we four,
Beneath the burden of the years, and praise the earth once more.

ALICE MEYNELL

1847–1922

A letter from a Girl to her own Old Age

Listen, and when thy hand this paper presses,
O time-worn woman, think of her who blesses
What thy thin fingers touch, with her caresses.

O mother, for the weight of years that break thee!
O daughter, for slow time must yet awake thee,
And from the changes of my heart must make thee!

O fainting traveller, morn is grey in heaven.
Dost thou remember how the clouds were driven?
And are they calm about the fall of even?

Pause near the ending of thy long migration,
For this one sudden hour of desolation
Appeals to one hour of thy meditation.

Suffer, O silent one, that I remind thee
Of the great hills that stormed the sky behind thee,
Of the wild winds of power that have resigned thee.

Know that the mournful plain where thou must wander
Is but a grey and silent world, but ponder
The misty mountains of the morning yonder.

Listen:- the mountain winds with rain were fretting,
And sudden gleams the mountain tops besetting.
I cannot let thee fade to death, forgetting.

What part of this wild heart of mine I know not
Will follow with thee where the great winds blow not,
And where the young flowers of the mountain grow not.

Yet let my letter with my lost thoughts in it
Tell what the way was when thou didst begin it,
And win with thee the goal when thou shalt win it.

Oh, in some hour of thine my thoughts shall guide thee,
Suddenly, though time, darkness, silence, hide thee,
This wind from thy lost country flits beside thee, −

Telling thee: all thy memories moved the maiden,
With thy regrets was morning over-shaden,
With sorrow, thou has left, her life was laden.

But whither shall my thoughts turn to pursue thee?
Life changes, and the years and days renew thee,
Oh, nature brings my straying heart unto thee.

Her winds will join us, with their constant kisses,
Upon the evening as the morning tresses,
Her summers breathe the same unchanging blisses.

And we, so altered in our shifting phases,
Track one another 'mid the many mazes
By the eternal child-breath of the daisies.

I have not writ this letter of divining
To make a glory of thy silent pining,
A triumph of thy mute and strange declining.

Only one youth, and the bright life was shrouded.
Only one morning, and the day was clouded.
And one old age with all regrets is crowded.

Oh, hush, Oh, hush! Thy tears my words are steeping,
Oh, hush, hush, hush! So full, the fount of weeping?
Poor eyes, so quickly moved, so near to sleeping?

Pardon the girl; such strange desires beset her.
Poor woman, lay aside the mournful letter
That breaks thy heart; the one who wrote, forget her:

The one who now thy faded features guesses,
With filial fingers thy grey hair caresses
With morning tears thy mournful twilight blesses.

WILLIAM WORDSWORTH

1770–1850

From *To a young Lady who has been reproached for taking long Walks in the Country*

> Thy thoughts and feelings shall not die,
> Not leave thee, when grey hairs are nigh,
> A melancholy slave;

But an old age, serene and bright,
And lovely as a Lapland night,
Shall lead thee to thy grave.

This poem was addressed to Dorothy Wordsworth as a young woman. She died aged eighty-four, having been for the last twenty years of her life a helpless invalid, physically infirm, her mind and memory gone.

ECCLESIASTES

Chapter 12, verses 1–7

Remember now thy Creator in the days of thy youth,
while the evil days come not, nor the years draw
nigh, when thou shalt say, I have no plesure in them;

While the sun, or the light, or the moon, or the stars,
be not darkened, nor the clouds return after the rain:

In the day when the keepers of the house shall tremble,
and the strong men shall bow themselves,
and the grinders cease because they are few,
and those that look out of the windows be darkened,

And the doors shall be shut in the streets, when
the sound of the grinding is low, and he shall rise
up at the voice of the bird, and all the daughters
of musick shall be brought low;

Also when they shall be afraid of that which is high,
and fears shall be the way, and the almond tree
shall flourish, and the grasshopper shall be a
burden, and desire shall fail: because man goeth
to his long home, and the mourners go about in the streets:

Or ever the silver cord be loosed, or the golden
bowl be broken, or the pitcher be broken at the
fountain, or the wheel broken at the cistern.

Then shall the dust return to the earth as it was:
and the spirit shall return unto God who gave it.

Young and old

WILLIAM SHAKESPEARE?

1564–1616

From *The Passionate Pilgrim*

Crabbed age and youth cannot live together;
Youth is full of pleasance, age is full of care;
Youth like summer morn, age like winter weather;
Youth like summer brave, age like winter bare.
Youth is full of sport, age's breath is short;
    Youth is nimble, age is lame;
Youth is hot and bold, age is weak and cold:
Youth is wild and age is tame.
Age, I do abhor thee; youth, I do adore thee;
    O! my love, my love is young:
Age, I do defy thee; O! sweet shepherd, hie thee,
    For methinks thou stay'st too long.

DYLAN THOMAS

1914–1953

Youth Calls to Age

You too have seen the sun a bird of fire
Stepping on clouds across the golden sky,
Have known man's envy and his weak desire,
Have loved and lost.
You, who are old, have loved and lost as I
All that is beautiful but born to die,
Have traced your patterns in the hastening frost.
And you have walked upon the hills at night,
And bared your head beneath the living sky,
When it was noon have walked into the light,
Knowing such joy as I.
Though there are years between us, they are naught;
Youth calls to age across the tired years:

'What have you found,' he cries, 'what have you sought?'
'What you have found,' age answers through his tears,
'What you have sought.'

ROBERT SOUTHEY

1774–1843

The Old Man's Comforts and How He Gained Them

'You are old, Father William,' the young man cried,
'The few locks which are left you are grey,
You are hale, Father William, a hearty old man,
Now tell me the reason, I pray.'

'In the days of my youth,' Father William replied,
'I remembered that youth would fly fast,
And abused not my health and my vigour at first
That I never might need them at last.'

'You are old, Father William,' the young man cried,
'And pleasures with youth pass away;
And yet you lament not the days that are gone,
Now tell me the reason, I pray.'

'In the days of my youth,' Father William replied,
'I remembered that youth could not last,
I thought of the future, whatever I did,
That I never might grieve for the past.'

'You are old, Father William,' the young man cried,
'And life must be hastening away;
You are cheerful, and love to converse upon death,
Now tell me the reason, I pray.'

'I am cheerful, young man,' Father William replied,
'Let the cause thy attention engage;
In the days of my youth I remembered my God!
And He hath not forgotten my age.'

LEWIS CARROLL (CHARLES DODGSON)

1832–1898

From *Alice in Wonderland. A parody of Southey*

'You are old, Father William,' the young man said,
    'And your hair has become very white:
And yet you incessantly stand on your head –
    Do you think, at your age, it is right?'

'In my youth,' Father William replied to his son,
    'I feared it might injure the brain;
But now that I'm perfectly sure I have none,
    Why, I do it again and again.'

'You are old,' said the youth, 'as I mentioned before,
    And have grown most uncommonly fat;
Yet you turned a back-somersault in at the door –
    Pray, what is the reason of that?'

'In my youth,' said the sage, as he shook his grey locks,
    'I kept all my limbs very supple
By the use of this ointment – one shilling the box –
    Allow me to sell you a couple?'

'You are old,' said the youth, 'and your jaws are too weak
    For anything tougher than suet;
Yet you finished the goose, with the bones and the beak –
    Pray how did you manage to do it?'

'In my youth,' said his father, 'I took to the law,
    And argued each case with my wife;
And the muscular strength which it gave to my jaw
    Has lasted the rest of my life.'

'You are old,' said the youth, 'one would hardly suppose
    That your eye was as steady as ever;
Yet you balanced an eel on the end of your nose –
    What made you so awfully clever?'

'I have answered three questions, and that is enough,'
   Said his father; 'don't give yourself airs!'
Do you think I can listen all day to such stuff?
   Be off, or I'll kick you down stairs!'

WILLIAM SHAKESPEARE

1564–1616

From *As You Like It, Act 2 Scene 3*

ORLANDO   What! Wouldst thou have me go and beg my food?
  Or with a base and boisterous sword enforce
  A thievish living on the common road?
  This must I do, or know not what to do . . .

ADAM   But do not so, I have five hundred crowns,
  The thrifty hire I saved under your father,
  Which I did store to be my foster-nurse
  When service should in my old limbs lie lame,
  And unregarded age in corners thrown.
  Take that: and He that doth the ravens feed,
  Yea, providently caters for the sparrow,
  Be comfort to my age! Here is the gold;
  All this I give you. Let me be your servant;
  Though I look old, yet I am strong and lusty:
  For in my youth I never did apply
  Hot and rebellious liquors in my blood,
  Nor did not with unbashful forehead woo
  The means of weakness and debility;
  Therefore my age is as a lusty winter,
  Frosty, but kindly, Let me go with you;
  I'll do the service of a younger man
  In all your business and necessities.

ORLANDO   O good old man; how well in thee appears
  The constant service of the antique world,
  When service sweat for duty, not for meed! . . .

ADAM   Master, go on, and I will follow thee
   To the last gasp with truth and loyalty.
   From seventeen years till now almost fourscore
   Here lived I, but now live here no more.
   At seventeen years many their fortunes seek;
   But at fourscore it is too late a week:
   Yet fortune cannot recompense me better
   Than to die well, and not my master's debtor.

WILLIAM WORDSWORTH

1770–1850

The Fountain; a Conversation

We talked with open heart, and tongue
Affectionate and true,
A pair of friends, though I was young,
And Matthew seventy-two.

We lay beneath a spreading oak,
Beside a mossy seat;
And from the turf a fountain broke,
And gurgled at our feet.

'Now Matthew!' said I, 'let us match
This water's pleasant tune
With some old border-song, or catch
That suits a summer's noon;

'Or of the church-clock and the chimes
Sing here beneath the shade,
That half-mad thing of witty rhymes
Which you last April made!'

In silence Matthew lay, and eyed
The spring beneath the tree;
And thus the dear old Man replied,
The grey-haired man of glee:

'No check, no stay, this Streamlet fears;
How merrily it goes!
'Twill murmur on a thousand years,
And flow as now it flows.

'And here, on this delightful day,
I cannot choose but think
How oft, a vigorous man, I lay
Beside this fountain's brink.

'My eyes are dim with childish tears,
My heart is idly stirred,
For the same sound is in my ears
Which in those days I heard.

'Thus fares it still in our decay:
And yet the wiser mind
Mourns less for what age takes away
Than what it leaves behind.

'The blackbird amid leafy trees,
The lark above the hill,
Let loose their carols when they please
Are quiet when they will.

'With Nature never do *they* wage
A foolish strife; they see
A happy youth, and their old age
Is beautiful and free:

'But we are pressed by heavy laws;
And often, glad no more,
We wear a face of joy, because
We have been glad of yore.

'If there be one who need bemoan
His kindred laid in earth,
The household hearts that were his own;
It is the man of mirth.

'My days, my Friend, are almost gone,
My life has been approved,
And many love me! but by none
Am I enough beloved.'

'Now both himself and me he wrongs,
The man who thus complains!
I live and sing my idle songs
Upon these happy plains;

'And Matthew, for thy children dead
I'll be a son to thee!'
At this he grasped my hand, and said,
'Alas, that cannot be.'

We rose up from the fountain-side;
And down the smooth descent
Of the green sheep-track did we glide;
And through the wood we went;

And, ere we came to Leonard's rock,
He sang those witty rhymes
About the crazy old church-clock,
And the bewildered chimes.

OLIVER WENDELL HOLMES

1809–1894

The Last Leaf

I saw him once before
As he pass'd by the door,
        And again
The pavement stone resound
As he totters o'er the ground
        With his cane.

They say that in his prime,
Ere the pruning-knife of Time
    Cut him down,
Not a better man was found
By the Crier on his round
    Through the town.

But now he walks the streets,
And he looks at all he meets
    Sad and wan,
And he shakes his feeble head,
That it seems as if he said,
    'They are gone'.

The mossy marbles rest
On his lips that he has prest
    In their bloom,
And the names he loved to hear
Have been carved for many a year
    On the tomb.

My grandmamma has said —
Poor old lady, she is dead
    Long ago —
That he had a Roman nose,
And his cheek was like a rose
    In the snow.

But now his nose is thin,
And it rests upon his chin
    Like a staff,
And a crook is in his back,
And a melancholy crack
    In his laugh.

I know it is a sin
For me to sit and grin
    At him here;
But the old three-corner'd hat,
And the breeches, and all that,
    Are so queer!

And if I should live to be
The last leaf upon the tree
    In the spring,
Let them smile, as I do now,
At the old forsaken bough
    Where I cling.

T'AO CH'IEN

372–427

Translated by Arthur Waley

Blaming Sons

(an apology for his own drunkenness)

White hair covers my temples,
I am wrinkled and gnarled beyond repair,
And though I have got five sons,
They all hate paper and brush.
A-Shu is sixteen;
For laziness there is none like him.
A-hsuian does his best,
But really loathes the Fine Arts.
Yung and Tuan are thirteen,
But do not know 'six' from 'seven'.
Tung- tzu in his ninth year
Is only concerned with things to eat.
If Heaven treats me like this,
What can I do but fill my cup?

MARGARET WALKER

1915–

Lineage

My grandmothers were strong.
They followed plows and bent to toil,

They moved through fields sowing seed,
They touched earth and grain grew,
They were full of sturdiness and singing.
My grandmothers were strong.

My grandmothers are full of memories.
Smelling of soap and onions and wet clay
With veins rolling roughly over quick hands
They have many clean words to say.
My grandmothers were strong.
Why am I not as they?

The author is a black American writer.

D. J. ENRIGHT

1920–

Geriatrics

I got on well with Granma.
Ours was the prescriptive relationship:
We used to play crib for hours, she gave me sweets,
She defended me, her I failed to defend.

It didn't worry me that she was getting
Troublesome. If she wandered in her mind a little,
So did I. Her husband was dead,
So was my father. The house had to be vacated.

We couldn't look after her, we were going
To look after a troublesome old man
Who at least had a house we could live in.
My eldest aunt declined to take her.

She would have to go to the Workhouse.
The worst thing was, they told her
She was going to a nursing-home for a while,
They even ordered a car.

She had to be pushed into it.
As the car moved off, I heard her
Shout with a dreadful new voice:
'I know where you're sending me,
You're sending me to the Workhouse!'

She was found to be deranged on arrival,
And they sent her on to another place,
So she didn't go to the workhouse after all,
She died soon after.

Granma doddered a bit,
But she was my friend.
Perhaps it had to be done
Did it have to be done like that?

It started me writing poems,
Unpleasant and enigmatic,
Which quite rightly no-one liked
But were thought to be 'modern'.

GUY BUTLER

1918–

Great-great-grandmother

Bolt upright, reading her Bible for hours
in a wicker chair on the front stoep in the winter,
in summer under the pepper trees whose lacy shadows
wavered over the lacy shawl
drawn tight across her little brittle shoulders.

When her sight grew dim someone might read to her –
but deafness following shut that door.
So then she'd sit, there, crocheting for hours
by a remnant of sight, and what sense of touch
was left in fingers as dry and silvery as silver leaves
freckled gold and brown.

But mostly her hands lay limp in her lap
except for occasional desperate twitches
which shook the shawl round her shoulder,
the shawl with which she seemed to shelter
her loneliness like a deformity
from a frightened and frightening world.

Alone. Husband and all her own children gone:
living among the noise of children's children
who found it hard to come near the awful
weak-eyed eagle of a race now almost extinct.
Sometimes, though, one of the wives in fumbling compassion
would make a child ask the old, old lady for a story.
She seldom obliged, reluctant to switch her mind
from her beginnings and endings to theirs.

But when she did her stories were mostly biblical
where the miraculous burst into the matter-of-fact
and weirdly wonderful was all mixed up
with things the child could see at once
were as they always are.

Or sometimes she'd talk of pioneer days, long treks,
locusts darkening the sky, assegai wounds
that would only heal to herbs that the Bushmen knew,
the coffin always ready in the loft, the frequent
births, betrothals, burials.

But rarely of her childhood over the water, among
hills called the Cotswolds, of things we never knew, like snow,
like chestnusts, and nightingales, whole hillsides
deep in perpetual lawn with not a stone to be seen,
trees, without thorns, as high as the house, things
as lovely, strange and barely credible
as chapters in the Bible.

Each sundown her custom was to go for a slow, slow walk
along the selfsame track that had brought her there
three score and all but ten years before,
her long mauve gown trailing a whiff of lavender

through miles of heady mimosa groves,
her cheek far softer and smoother
than any wild petal or fruit.

I was a young savage then, forever
chasing rats and lizards with my catty.
Springtime it was – what passes for spring up there –
that gradual crescendo of heat with little change or colour,
that thorough dessication of air
before the great clouds stride across the sky
meet growling, and sighing fall.

The blue-headed lizard flicked his tail
and my futile pebble clicked on his purple boulder.
Released from their fatal focus, my eyes drifted up
and there she was, not fifty yards away, stock-still, black,
next to a wild pomegranite, flaming yellow, intense
against the funereal mauves of the scrub.

Was she resting, or dreaming, or peering with lashless eyes
at that annual but always suprising outburst of yellow?
And then, behind her, I saw the whirlwind coming;
now lurching like an inspired dancer
who snatches a beautiful moment
from the verge of a hideous fall,
now stalking straight and poised
like the holy pillar of smoke that led the Israelites
into the Promised Land.

She did not hear or see it come.

It struck her and she was gone.

For a dizzy split second I thought:
She's been taken up to heaven, like Elijah!
And her shawl spun out of the sky and settled beside me.
Was I Elisha, inheriting
her mantle of powerful pain?
But then I saw her dress like a gnarled old branch
Black in the flame of the bush.

I ran up crying, trying to help her.
But she sized things up, as always;
she never lost her head.
'Go to the house. Fetch Thomas'

In her fall she had clutched at the thorny branches.
That's how the palms of her hands were pierced.

She was three long weeks a-dying.

There were times when she struggled to speak,
but it was too late, tetanus being what it is.

They buried her between two thunderstorms.
The scent the damp earth breathed
from the parted lips of her grave
was neither bitter nor sweet.

I did not weep then;
it is now that I weep.

Guy Butler is a white South African of English descent.

C. DAY LEWIS

1904–1972

From *My Mother's Sister*

. . . – Who, her sister dying, took on the four-year
Child, and the chance that now she would never make
A child of her own; who, mothering me, flowered in
The clover-soft authority of the meek.

Who, exiled, gossiping home chat from abroad
In roundhand letters to a drift of relations –
Squires', Goldsmiths, Overends, Williams' – sang the songs
Of Zion in a strange land. Hers the patience

Of one who made no claims, but simply loved
Because that was her nature, and loving so
Asked no more than to be repaid in kind.
If she was not a saint, I do not know

What saints are . . .

. . . Now sunk in one small room of a Rathmines
Old people's home, helpless, beyond speech
Or movement, yearly deeper she declines
To imbecility – my last link with childhood.

The battery's almost done; yet if I press
The button hard – some private joke in boyhood
I teased her with – there comes upon her face
A glowing of the old, enchanted smile.

So, still alive, she rots. A heart of granite
Would melt at this unmeaning sequel. Lord,
How can this be justified, how can it
Be justified?

DYLAN THOMAS

1914–1953

*Do not go gentle into
that good night*

Do not go gentle into that good night,
Old age should burn and rave at close of day;
Rage, rage against the dying of the light.

Though wise men at their end know dark is right,
Because their words had forked no lightning they
Do not go gentle into that good night.

Good men, the last wave by, crying how bright
Their frail deeds might have danced in a green bay,
Rage, rage against the dying of the light.

Wild men who caught and sang the sun in flight,
And learn, too late, they grieved it on its way,
Do not go gentle into that good night.

Grave men, near death, who see with blinding sight
Blind eyes could blaze like meteors and be gay,
Rage, rage against the dying of the light.

And you, my father, there on the sad height,
Curse, bless, me now with your fierce tears, I pray,
Do not go gentle into that good night.
Rage, rage against the dying of the light.

CHRISTINA ROSSETTI

1830–1894

Valentines to my Mother

I   1876

Fairer than younger beauties, more beloved
　　Than many a wife,
By stress of Time's vicissitudes unmoved
　　From settled calm of life;

Endearing rectitude to those who watch
　　The verdict of your face,
Raising and making gracious those who catch
　　A semblance of your grace:

With kindly lips of welcome, and with pleased
　　Propitious eyes benign,
Accept a kiss of homage from your least,
　　Last Valentine.

II   1882

My blessed mother dozing in her chair
On Christmas Day seemed an embodied Love,
A comfortable Love with soft brown hair
Softened and silvered to a tint of dove;
A better sort of Venus with an air
Angelical from thoughts that dwell above;
A wiser Pallas in whose body fair
Enshrined a blessed soul looks out thereof.
Winter brought holly then; now Spring has brought
Paler and frailer snowdrops shivering;
And I have brought a simple humble thought –
I her devoted duteous Valentine –
A lifelong thought which thrills this song I sing,
A lifelong love to this dear Saint of mine.

GEORGE BARKER

1913–1991

To my Mother

Most near, most dear, most loved and most far,
Under the window where I often found her
Sitting as huge as Asia, seismic with laughter,
Gin and chicken helpless in her Irish hand,
Irresistible as Rabelais, but most tender for
The lame dogs and hurt birds that surround her –
She is a procession no one can follow after
But be like a little dog following a brass band.

She will not glance up at the bomber, or condescend
To drop her gin and scuttle to a cellar,
But lean on the mahogany table like a mountain
Whom only faith can move, and so I send
O all my faith, and all my love to tell her
That she will move from mourning into morning.

W.B. YEATS

1865–1939

The Song of the Old Mother

I rise in the dawn, and I kneel and blow
Till the seed of the fire flicker and glow;
And then I must scrub and bake and sweep
Till stars are beginning to blink and peep;
And the young lie long and dream in their bed
Of the matching of ribbons for bosom and head,
And their day goes over in idleness,
And they sigh if the wind but lift a tress:
While I must work because I am old,
And the seed of the fire gets feeble and cold.

MARGARET CROPPER

1866–1980

I'll Hold your Hand

They were unkind steps, no rail for the old and shaken,
And there they lay. Most days, on my way home,
They brought me to a stand – a halting moment;
'If you should fall,' they said, 'if you should fall.'
I was standing there feeling rather fearful and old,
When I heard a voice behind me, a childish voice,
Almost too soft to be heard, and into my hand
A very small hand came, peacefully holding mine.
It was such a small hand, a six year old hand perhaps,
Holding my withered fingers in innocent grasp;
It was matched by the sweetest voice, and the confident message:
'I'll hold your hand till you get down those steps.'
I don't think I could have fallen after that;
It would have been blasphemy to think of falling;
So step by step I went hopefully to the road.

54

I dared then to look round, but the child had vanished;
I never saw her – but something stirred in me,
Someone had come, someone had come to help me.

CHRISTINA ROSSETTI

1830–1894

Dedicatory Sonnet

Sonnets are full of love, and this my tome
Has many sonnets; so here now shall be
One sonnet more, a love sonnet, from me
To her whose heart is my heart's quiet home,
To my first Love, my Mother, on whose knee
I learnt love-lore that is not troublesome;
Whose service is my special dignity,
And she my loadstar while I go and come.
And so because you love me, and because
I love you, Mother, I have woven a wreath
Of rhymes, wherewith to crown your honoured name;
In you not fourscore years can dim the flame
Of love, whose blessed glow transcends the laws
Of time and change and mortal life and death.

FRANCES CORNFORD

1886–1960

Childhood

I used to think that grown-up people chose
To have stiff backs and wrinkles round their nose
And veins like small fat snakes on either hand,
On purpose to be grand,
Till through the banisters I watched one day
My great-aunt Etty's friend who was going away,

And how her onyx beads had come unstrung,
I saw her grope to find them as they rolled;
and then I knew that she was helplessly old,
As I was helplessly young.

'Beauty vanishes, beauty passes'

MATTHEW PRIOR

1664–1721

To a Lady who offers her Looking-Glass to Venus

Venus, take my votive glass:
Since I am not what I was,
What from this day I shall be,
Venus, let me never see.

CHRISTINA ROSSETTI

1830–1894

Passing and Glassing

All things that pass
Are woman's looking-glass;
They show her how her bloom must fade,
And she herself be laid
With withered roses in the shade;
    With withered roses and the fallen peach,
    Unlovely, out of reach
      Of summer joy that was.

All things that pass
Are woman's tiring-glass
The faded lavender is sweet,
Sweet the dead violet
Culled and laid by and cared for yet;
    The dried-up violets and dried lavender
    Still sweet, may comfort her,
      Nor need she cry Alas!

All things that pass
Are wisdom's looking-glass;
Being full of hope and fear, and still
Brimful of good or ill,

According to our work and will;
For there is nothing new beneath the sun;
Our doings have been done,
And that which shall be was.

SAMUEL DANIEL

1562–1619

Sonnet to Delia

Beauty, sweet Love, is like the morning dew,
Whose short refresh upon the tender green
Cheers for a time, but till the sun doth shew,
And straight 'tis gone as it had never been.
Soon doth it fade that makes the fairest flourish,
Short is the glory of the blushing rose,
The hue which thou so carefully dost nourish,
Yet which at length thou must be forced to lose.
When thou, surcharged with burdens of thy years,
Shall bend thy wrinkles homeward to the earth,
And that in beauty's lease expired appears
The date of age, the calends of our death –
But ah! no more; this must not be foretold,
For women grieve to think they must be old.

FROM THE GREEK ANTHOLOGY
TRANSLATED BY HUMBERT WOLFE

1886–1940

Prodike. (Original by Rufinus)

Did I not say: 'We'll wither, We shall see
how soon! love's dissolutions, Prodike?
Wrinkles, grey hair, and all the perfidies
of face and form?' And now who seeks your kiss?

And who beseeches in its gathering gloom
your beauty, lonely as a wayside tomb?

The Nemesis of Love. (Original by Agathias)

She who was lovely, but as proud as fair,
tossing the woven glories of her hair,
who mocked my grief, strays now a withered ghost
mourning her loveliness for ever lost.
Where are the snows that were her breasts? the wonder
men called her voice? her brows', her eyelids' splendour?
Gone with grey hairs, love's Nemesis, that must
bring all things fair, but first the proud, to dust.

RUDYARD KIPLING

1865–1936

The Looking-Glass

Queen Bess was Harry's Daughter!

The Queen was in her chamber, and she was middling old,
Her petticoat was satin and her stomacher was gold.
Backwards and forwards and sideways did she pass,
Making up her mind to face the cruel looking-glass.
    The cruel looking-glass that will never show a lass
    As comely or as kindly or as young as once she was.

The Queen was in her chamber, a-combing of her hair,
There came Queen Mary's spirit and it stood behind her chair,
Singing, 'Backwards and forwards and sideways may you pass,
But I will stand behind you till you face the looking-glass,
    The cruel looking-glass that will never show a lass
    As lovely or unlucky or as lonely as I was!'

The Queen was in her chamber, a-weeping very sore,
There came Lord Leicester's spirit and it scratched upon the door,
Singing, 'Backwards and forwards and sideways may you pass,

But I will walk beside you till you face the looking-glass,
 The cruel looking-glass that will never show a lass
 As hard and unforgiving or as wicked as you was!'

The Queen was in her chamber; her sins were on her head;
She looked the spirits up and down and statelily she said;
'Backwards and forwards and sideways though I've been,
Yet I am Harry's daughter and I am England's Queen!'
 And she faced the looking-glass (and whatever else there was),
 And she saw her day was over and she saw her beauty pass
 In the cruel looking-glass that can always hurt a lass
 More hard than any ghost there is or any man there was!

WANG WEI

699–761

Translated by G.W. Robinson

Sitting Alone on an Autumn Night

I sit alone sad at my whitening hair
Waiting for ten o'clock in my empty house;
In the rain the hill fruits fall,
Under my lamp the grasshoppers sound.
White hairs will never be transformed;
That elixir is beyond creation.
To eliminate decrepitude
Study the Absolute.

ROBERT HERRICK

1591–1674

Upon Wrinkles

Wrinkles no more are, or no less,
Than beauty turned to sourness.

WILLIAM SHAKESPEARE

1564–1616

Sonnet LXXVII

Thy glass will show thee how thy beauties wear,
Thy dial how thy precious minutes waste;
The vacant leaves thy mind's imprint will bear,
And of this book this learning mayst thou taste.
The wrinkles which thy glass will truly show
Of mouthed graves will give thee memory;
Thou by thy dial's shady stealth mayst know
Time's thievish progress to eternity.
Look! What thy memory cannot contain,
Commit to these waste blanks, and thou shalt find
Those children nursed, deliver'd from thy brain,
To take a new acquaintance of thy mind.
    These offices, so oft as thou wilt look,
    Shall profit thee, and much enrich thy book.

WALTER DE LA MARE

1873–1956

Age

This ugly old crone –
Every beauty she had
When a maid, when a maid.
Her beautiful eyes,
Too youthful, too wise,
Seemed ever to come
To so lightless a home,
Cold and dull as a stone.
And her cheeks – who would guess
Cheeks cadaverous as this
Once with colours were gay
As the flower on its spray?

Who would ever believe
Aught could bring one to grieve
So much as to make
Lips bent for love's sake
So thin and so grey?
O Youth, come away!
All she asks is her lone,
This old, desolate crone.
She loves us no more;
She is too old to care
For the charms that of yore
Made her body so fair.
Past ripening, past care,
She lives but to bear
One or two fleeting years
Earth's indifference; her tears
Have lost now their heat;
Her hands and her feet
Now shake but to be
Shed as leaves from a tree;
And her poor heart beats on
Like a sea – the storm gone.

ANON.

1744

Epitaph on the Duchess of Marlborough

In former courts polite and gay,
And still a beauty in decay,
Go mourn in form, yet shed no tears,
Such falls give life to happy heirs.
Who can lament a full ripe death
When eighty-five resigns its breath?
So plums in autumn's fruitful crop,
Mellowed by time, corrupt and drop.

WILLIAM WORDSWORTH

1770–1850

To . . . in her Seventieth Year

Such age how beautiful! O Lady bright
Whose mortal lineaments seem all refined
By favouring Nature and a saintly Mind
To something purer and more exquisite
Than flesh and blood; whenever thou meet'st my sight,
When I behold thy blanched unwithered cheek,
Thy temples fringed with locks of gleaming white
And head that droops because the soul is meek,
Thee with the welcome Snowdrop I compare;
That child of winter, prompting thoughts that climb
From desolation toward the genial prime;
Or with the Moon, conquering earth's misty air,
And filling more and more with crystal light
As pensive Evening deepens into night.

JOSEPH CAMPBELL

1879–1944

The Old Woman

As a white candle
In a holy place,
So is the beauty
Of an aged face.

As the spent radiance
Of the winter sun,
So is a woman
With her travail done.

Her brood gone from her,
And her thoughts as still
As the waters
Under a ruined mill.

CH'EN CHIEH

1274

Translated by Robert Kotewell and Norman L. Smith

Wind of Spring

You touch the Willows, and make a new green;
You breathe on the peaches, and restore a pristine red;
But for my fading countenance and my greying hair
I dare not blame you, O East Wind

THOMAS RANDOLPH

1605–1635

Upon his Picture

When age has made me what I am not now;
And every wrinkle tells me where the plough
Of time hath furrowed; when an ice shall flow
Through every vein, and all my head wear snow;
When death displays his coldness in my cheek
And I myself in my own picture seek,
Not finding what I am, but what I was,
In doubt which to believe, this or my glass;
Yet though I alter, this remains the same
As it was drawn, retains the primitive frame
And first complexion; here will still be seen
Blood on the cheek, and down upon the chin.
Here the smooth brow will stay, the lively eye,
The ruddy lip, and hair of youthful dye.

66

Behold what frailty we in man may see
Whose shadow is less given to change than he.

Thomas Randolph died at the age of thirty.

WILLIAM WORDSWORTH

1770–1850

To a Painter

All praise the Likeness by thy skill portrayed;
But 'tis the fruitless task to paint for me,
Who, yielding not to changes Time has made,
By the habitual light of memory see
Eyes unbedimmed, see bloom that cannot fade,
And smiles that from their birthplace ne'er shall flee
Into the land where ghosts and phantoms be;
And, seeing this, own nothing in its stead.
Couldst thou go back into far-distant years,
And share with me, fond thought! that inward eye,
Then, and then only, Painter! could thy Art
The visual powers of Nature satisfy,
Which hold, whate'er to common sight appears,
Their sovereign empire in a faithful heart.

On the same Subject

Though I beheld at first with blank surprise
This Work, I now have gazed on it so long
I see its truth with unreluctant eyes;
O, my Beloved! I have done thee wrong,
Conscious of blessedness, but, whence it sprung,
Ever too heedless, as I now perceive:
Morn into noon did pass, noon into eve,
And the old day was welcome as the young,
As welcome, and as beautiful – in sooth
More beautiful, as being a thing more holy:
Thanks to thy virtues, to the eternal youth

Of all thy goodness, never melancholy;
To thy large heart and humble mind, that cast
Into one vision, future, present, past.

JOHN DONNE

1572–1631

The Autumnal

No spring, nor summer beauty hath such grace,
    As I have seen in one autumnal face.
Young beauties force our love, and that's a rape,
    This doth but counsel, yet you cannot scape.
If t'were a shame to love, here t'were no shame,
    Affection here takes Reverence's name;
Were her first years the Golden Age; that's true,
    But now she's gold oft tried, and ever new.
That was her torrid and inflaming time,
    This is her tolerable tropic clime.
Fair eyes, who asks more heat than comes from hence,
    He in a fever wishes pestilence.
Call not these wrinkles graves; if graves they were,
    They were Love's graves; for else he is no where.
Yet lies not Love dead here, but here doth sit
    Vowed to this trench, like an anchorite.
And here, till hers, which must be his death, come,
    He doth not dig a grave, but build a tomb.
Here dwells he, though he sojourn everywhere,
    In progress, yet his standing house is here.
Here, where still evening is; not noon, nor night;
    Where no voluptuousness, yet all delight.
In all her words, unto all hearers fit,
    You may at revels, you at counsel, sit.
This is Love's timber, youth his under-wood;
    There he, as wine in June, enrages blood,
Which then comes seasonabliest, when our taste
    And appetite to other things, is past.

Xerxes strange Lydian love, the platane tree,
   Was loved for age, none being so large as she,
Or else because, being young, nature did bless
   Her youth with age's glory, barrenness.
If we love things long sought, age is a thing
   Which we are fifty years in compassing;
If transitory things, which soon decay,
   Age must be loveliest at the latest day.
But name not winter-faces, whose skin's slack;
   Lank, as an unthrift's purse; but a soul's sack;
Whose eyes seek light within, for all here's shade;
   Whose mouths are holes, rather worn out, than made;
Whose every tooth to a several place is gone,
   To vex their souls at resurrection;
Name not these living deaths-heads unto me,
   For these not ancient, but antique be.
I hate extremes; yet I had rather stay
   With tombs, than cradles, to wear out a day.
Since such loves natural lation* is, may still
   My love descend, and journey down the hill,
Not panting after growing beauties, so,
   I shall ebb out with them, who home-ward go.

* A rare astronomical term meaning 'local motion from one place to another'.

GERARD MANLEY HOPKINS

1844–1889

The Leaden Echo and the Golden Echo

THE LEADEN ECHO

How to keep – is there any, any, is there none such, nowhere known
  some, bow or brooch or braid or brace, lace, latch or catch or key to
  keep
Back beauty, keep it, beauty, beauty, beauty . . . from vanishing away?

O is there no frowning of these wrinkles, ranked wrinkles deep,
Down? no waving off of these most mournful messengers, still
    messengers, sad and stealing messengers of grey?
No there's none, there's none, O no there's none,
Nor can you long be, what you now are, called fair,
Do what you may do, what, do what you may,
And wisdom is early to despair:
Be beginning; since, no, nothing can be done
To keep at bay
Age and age's evils, hoar hair,
Ruck and wrinkle, drooping, dying, death's worst, winding sheets,
    tombs and worms and tumbling to decay;
So be beginning, be beginning to despair,
O there's none; no no no there's none:
Be beginning to despair, to despair,
Despair, despair, despair, despair.

THE GOLDEN ECHO

    Spare!
There is one, yes I have one (Hush there!);
Only not within seeing of the sun,
Not within the singeing of the strong sun,
Tall sun tingeing, or treacherous the tainting of the earth's air,
Somewhere elsewhere there is ah well where! one,
One. Yes I can tell such a key, I do know such a place,
Where whatever's prized and passes of us, everything that's fresh and
    fast flying of us, seems to us sweet of us and swiftly away with done
    away with, undone,
Undone, done with, soon done with, and yet dearly and dangerously
    sweet
Of us, the wimpled-water-dimpled, not-by-morning-matched face,
The flower of beauty, fleece of beauty, too too apt to ah! to fleet,
Never fleets more, fastened with the tenderest truth
To its own best being and its loveliness of youth: it is an
    everlastingness of, O it is an all youth!
Come then, your ways and airs and looks, locks, maiden gear, gallantry
    and gaiety and grace,
Winning ways, airs innocent, maiden manners, sweet looks, loose
    locks, long locks, lovelocks, gaygear, going gallant, girlgrace –

Resign them, sign them, seal them, send them, motion them with
   breath,
And with sighs soaring, soaring sighs deliver
Them; beauty-in-the-ghost, deliver it, early now, long before death
Give beauty back, beauty, beauty, beauty, back to God, beauty's self
   and beauty's giver.
See; not a hair is, not an eyelash, not the least lash lost; every hair
Is, hair of the head, numbered.
Nay, what we had lighthanded left in surly the mere mould
Will have waked and have waxed and have walked with the wind
   what while we slept,
This side, that side hurling a heavyheaded hundredfold
What while we, while we slumbered.
O then, weary then why should we tread? O why are we so haggard at
   the heart, so care-coiled, care-killed, so fagged, so fashed, so cogged,
   so cumbered,
When the thing we freely forfeit is kept with fonder a care,
Fonder a care kept than we could have kept it, kept
Far with fonder a care (and we, we should have lost it) finer, fonder
A care kept, – Where kept? Do but tell us where kept, where, –
Yonder. – What high as that! We follow, now we follow, –
   Yonder, yes yonder, yonder,
Yonder.

Husband and wife

ROBERT BURNS

1759–1796

John Anderson, my Jo

John Anderson, my jo, John,
    When we were first acquent,
Your locks were like the raven,
    Your bonnie brow was brent;
But now your brow is beld, John,
    Your locks are like the snow;
But blessings on your frosty pow,
    John Anderson, my jo!

John Anderson, my jo, John,
    We clamb the hill thegither;
And monie a canty day, John,
    We've had we' ane anither;
Now we maun totter down, John,
    But hand in hand we'll go,
And sleep thegither at the foot,
    John Anderson, my jo.

ELIZABETH JENNINGS

1926–

One Flesh

Lying apart now, each in a separate bed,
He with a book, keeping the light on late,
She like a girl dreaming of childhood,
All men elsewhere – it is as if they wait
Some new event; the book he holds unread,
Her eyes fixed on the shadows overhead.

Tossed up like flotsam from a former passion,
How cool they lie. They hardly ever touch,
Or if they do it is like a confession
Of having little feeling – or too much.
Chastity faces them, a destination
For which their whole loves were a preparation.

Strangely apart, yet strangely close together,
Silence between them like a thread to hold
And not wind in. And time's itself's a feather
Touching them gently. Do they know they're old,
Those two who are my father and my mother
Whose fire from which I came, has now grown cold?

F. PRATT GREEN

1903–

The Old Couple

The old couple in the brand-new bungalow,
Drugged with the milk of municipal kindness,
Fumble their way to bed. Oldness at odds
With newness, they nag each other to show
Nothing is altered, despite the strangeness
Of being divorced in sleep by twin-beds,
Side by side like the Departed, above them
The grass-green of candlewick bedspreads.

In a dead neighbourhood, where it is rare
For hooligans to shout or dogs to bark,
A footfall in the quiet air is crisper
Than home-made bread; and the budgerigar
Bats an eyelid, as sensitive to disturbance
As a distant needle is to an earthquake
In the Great Deep, then balances in sleep.
It is silence keeps the old couple awake.

Too old for loving now, but not for love,
The old couple lie, several feet apart.
Their chesty breathing like a muted duet
On wind instruments, trying to think of
Things to hang on to, such as the tinkle
That a budgerigar makes when it shifts
Its feather weight from one leg to another,
The way, on windy nights, linoleum lifts.

JOHN BETJEMAN

1906–1984

House of Rest

Now all the world she knew is dead
    In this small room she lives her days,
The wash-hand stand and single bed
    Screened from the public gaze.

The horse-brass shines, the kettle sings,
    The cup of China tea
Is tasted among cared-for things
    Ranged round for me to see –

Lincoln, by Valentine and Co.,
    Now yellowish brown and stained,
But there some fifty years ago
    Her Harry was ordained;

Outside the church at Woodhall Spa
    The smiling groom and bride,
And here's his old tobacco jar
    Dried lavender inside.

I do not like to ask if he
    Was 'High' or 'Low' or 'Broad'
Lest such a question seem to be
    A mockery of Our Lord.

Her full grey eyes look far beyond
  The little room and me
To village church and village pond
  And ample rectory.

She sees her children each in place
  Eyes downcast as they wait,
She hears her Harry murmur Grace,
  Then heaps the porridge plate.

Aroused at seven, to bed by ten,
  They fully lived each day,
Dead sons, so motor-bike-mad then,
  And daughters far away.

Now when the bells for Eucharist
  Sound in the market Square,
With sunshine struggling through the mist
  And Sunday in the air.

The veil between her and her dead
  Dissolves and shows them clear,
The Consecration Prayer is said
  And all of them are near.

WALTER DE LA MARE

1873–1956

Old Ben

Sad is old Ben Thistlewaite,
  Now his day is done,
And all his children
  Far away and gone.

He sits beneath his jasmined porch,
  His stick between his knees,
His eyes fixed, vacant,
  On his moss-grown trees.

Grass springs in the green path,
   His flowers are lean and dry,
His thatch hangs in wisps against
   The evening sky.

He has no heart to care now,
   Though the winds will blow
Whistling in his casement,
   And the rain drip through.

He thinks of his old Bettie,
   How she would shake her head and say,
'You'll live to wish my sharp tongue
   Could scold – some day'.

But as in pale high autumn skies
   The swallows float and play,
His restless thoughts pass to and fro,
   But nowhere stay.

Soft, on the morrow, they are gone;
   His garden then will be
Denser and shadier and greener,
   Greener the moss-grown tree.

THOMAS HARDY

1840–1928

Wives in the Sere

Never a careworn wife but shows,
   If a joy suffuse her,
Something beautiful to those
   Patient to peruse her,
Some one charm the world unknows
   Precious to a muser,
Haply what, ere years were foes,
   Moved her mate to choose her.

But, be it a hint of rose
    That an instant hues her,
Or some early light or pose
    Wherewith thought renews her –
Seen by him as full, ere woes
    Practised to abuse her –
Sparely comes it, swiftly goes,
    Time again subdues her.

RUPERT BROOKE

1887–1915

Menelaus and Helen

I

Hot through Troy's ruin Menelaus broke
    To Priam's palace, sword in hand, to sate
    On that adulterous whore a ten years' hate
And a king's honour. Through red death and smoke,
And cries, and then by quieter ways he strode,
    Till the still innermost chamber fronted him.
    He swung his sword, and crashed into the dim
Luxurious bower, flaming like a god.

High sat white Helen, lonely and serene,
    He had not remembered that she was as fair
And that her neck curved down in such a way;
And he felt tired; he flung the sword away,
    And kissed her feet, and knelt before her there,
The perfect knight before the perfect Queen.

II

So far the poet. How should he behold
    That journey home, the long connubial years?
    He does not tell you how white Helen bears
Child on legitimate child, becomes a scold,
Haggard with virtue. Menelaus bold
    Waxed garrulous, and sacked a hundred Troys

'Twixt noon and supper. And her golden voice
Got shrill as he grew deafer. And both were old.

Often he wonders why on earth he went
   Troyward, or why poor Paris ever came.
Oft she weeps, gummy-eyed and impotent;
   Her dry shanks twitch at Paris' mumbled name.
So Menelaus nagged; and Helen cried;
And Paris slept on by Scamander's side

THOMAS HARDY

1840–1928

Faithful Wilson

'I say she's handsome, by all laws
Of beauty, if wife ever was!'
Wilson insists thus, though each day
The years fret Fanny towards decay.
'She *was* once beautiful as a jewel,'
Hint friends; 'but Time, of course, is cruel'.
Still Wilson does not feel quite how,
Once fair, she can be different now.

Partly from Strato of Sardis

GEORGE CRABBE

1754–1832

A Marriage Ring

The ring, so worn as you behold,
So thin, so pale, is yet of gold:
The passion such it was to prove –
Worn with life's care, love yet was love.

The last two poems in this section illustrate that pleasant and fairly common relationship between a man and a woman, who may or may not have been lovers in their youth, but live together happily in old age. Crabbe's poem makes clear that his couple had never been lovers; Cowper lived for thirty years in Mary Unwin's home, first as lodger, then as friend, without a hint of scandal touching their close but innocent relationship.

GEORGE CRABBE

1754–1832

From *The Parting Hour*

Beneath yon tree, observe an ancient pair —
A sleeping man; a woman in her chair,
Watching his looks with kind and pensive air;
No wife, nor sister she, nor is the name
Nor kindred of this friendly pair the same;
Yet so allied are they, that few can feel
Her constant, warm, unwearied, anxious zeal;
Their years and woes, although they long have loved,
Keep their good name and conduct unreproved;
Thus life's small comforts they together share,
And while life lingers for the grave prepare.

WILLIAM COWPER

1731–1800

My Mary

The twentieth year is wellnigh past
Since first our sky was overcast;
Ah, would that this might be the last!
                    My Mary!

The spirits have a fainter flow,
I see thee daily weaker grow;
Twas my distress that brought thee low,
                    My Mary!

Thy needles, once a shining store,
For my sake restless heretofore,
Now rust disused, and shine no more;
                    My Mary!

For though thou gladly wouldst fulfil
The same kind office for me still,
Thy sight now seconds not thy will,
                    My Mary!

But well thou play'dst the housewife's part,
And all thy threads with magic art
Have wound themselves about this heart,
                    My Mary!

Thy indistinct expressions seem
Like language utter'd in a dream;
Yet me they charm whate'er the theme,
                    My Mary!

Thy silver locks, once auburn bright,
Are still more lovely in my sight
Than golden beams of orient light,
                    My Mary!

For could I view nor them nor thee,
What sight worth seeing could I see?
The sun would rise in vain for me,
                    My Mary!

Partakers of thy sad decline,
Thy hands their little force resign;
Yet, gently press'd, press gently mine,
                    My Mary!

Such feebleness of limb thou prov'st
That now at every step thou mov'st
Upheld by two; yet still thou lov'st,
                    My Mary!

And still to love, though press'd with ill,
In wintry age to feel no chill,
With me is to be lovely still,
                    My Mary!

But ah – by constant heed I know
How oft the sadness that I show
Transforms thy smiles to looks of woe,
                    My Mary!

And should my future lot be cast
With much resemblance of the past,
Thy worn-out heart will break at last –
                    My Mary!

Old friends

WILLIAM (JOHNSON) CORY

1823–1892

Heraclitus

They told me, Heraclitus, they told me you were dead,
They brought me bitter news to hear and bitter tears to shed.
I wept as I remember'd how often you and I
Had tired the sun with talking and sent him down the sky.

And now that you art lying, my dear old Carian guest,
A handful of grey ashes, long long ago at rest,
Still are thy pleasant voices, thy nightingales, awake;
For Death, he taketh all way, but them he cannot take.

PO CHU-I

A.D. 772–846

Translated by Arthur Waley

Separation

Yesterday I heard that such-a-one was gone;
This morning they tell me that so-and-so is dead.
Of friends and acquaintances more than two-thirds
Have suffered change and passed to the Land of Ghosts.
Those that are gone I shall not see again;
They, alas, are forever finished and done.
These that are left – where are they now?
They are all scattered, – a thousand miles away.
Those I have known and loved through all my life,
On the fingers of my hand, – how many do I count?
Only the prefects of T'ung, Kuo and Li
And Feng Province – just those four.
Longing for each other we are all grown gray;
Through the Fleeting World rolled like a wave in the stream.

Alas that the feasts and frolics of old days
Have withered and vanished, bringing us to this!
When shall we meet and drink a cup of wine
And laughing gaze into each other's eyes?

CHARLES LAMB

1774–1834

The Old Familiar Faces

I have had playmates, I have had companions,
In my days of childhood, in my joyful school-days –
All, all are gone, the old familiar faces.

I have been laughing, I have been carousing,
Drinking late, sitting late, with my bosom cronies –
All, all are gone, the old familiar faces.

I loved a Love once, fairest among women:
Closed are her doors on me, I must not see her –
All, all are gone, the old familiar faces..

I have a friend, a kinder friend has no man:
Like an ingrate, I left my friend abruptly;
Left him, to muse on the old familiar faces.

Ghost-like I paced round the haunts of my childhood,
Earth seemed a desert I was bound to traverse,
Seeking to find the old familiar faces.

Friend of my bosom, thou more than a brother,
Why were thou not born in my father's dwelling?
So we might talk of the old familiar faces –

How some have died, and some they have left me,
And some are taken from me; all are departed –
All, all are gone, the old familiar faces.

DAVID HOPKINSON

1914–

Friends of Old Age

Some have enacted death;
It makes no odds, for all
Circle around my head
Alive or dead.

They are contained within
The hovel I have built;
They deserved palaces
But still have faces.

Therefore my will persists
In netting these dear fish
To swim in the mind's eye
Until I die.

Feebly I hold them all
Within the mind's embrace;
Each other they may greet
But never meet.

Mustered within my head
All whom I love distil
Sweet vapour in the air
Stifling despair.

They form while light persists
An antidote to torpor
And carry me across
Impending loss.

They underwrite my days,
Restore all I once owned;
Their presence in my age
Unfastens rage,

Transposes thought from dust
To browse in upper air
Among the good and true
Whom once I knew.

JAMES THOMSON

1700–1748

On the Death of a particular Friend

As those we love decay, we die in part,
String after string is sever'd from the heart;
Till loosened life, at last but breathing clay,
Without one pang is glad to fall away.

Unhappy he who latest feels the blow!
Whose eyes have wept o'er every friend laid low,
Dragg'd lingering on from partial death to death,
Till, dying, all he can resign is – breath.

ALEXANDER POPE

1688–1744

From *The Essay on Man*

Heav'n forming each on other to depend,
A master, or a servant, or a friend,
Bids each on other for assistance call,
'Till one Man's weakness grows the strength of all.
Wants, frailties, passions, closer still ally
The common int'rest, or endear the tie.
To these we owe true friendship, love sincere,
Each home-felt joy that life inherits here;
Yet from the same we learn, in its decline,
Those joys, those loves, those int'rests to resign;
Taught half by reason, half by mere decay,
To welcome death, and calmly pass away.

EDWARD FITZGERALD

1809–1883

Old Song

'Tis a dull sight
  To see the year dying,
When winter winds
  Set the yellow wood sighing:
    Sighing, O sighing!

When such a time cometh
  I do retire
Into an old room
  Beside a bright fire:
    O, pile a bright fire!

And there I sit
  Reading old things,
Of knights and lorn damsels,
  While the wind sings –
    O, drearily sings!

I never look out
  Or attend to the blast,
For all to be seen
  Is the leaves falling fast:
    Falling, falling!

But close at the hearth,
  Like a cricket, sit I,
Reading of summer
  And chivalry –
    Gallant chivalry!

Then with an old friend
  I talk of our youth –
How 'twas gladsome, but often
  Foolish, forsooth:
    But gladsome, gladsome!

91

Or, to get merry,
   We sing some old rhyme
That made the wood ring again
   In summer time –
     Sweet Summer time!

Then go we smoking,
   Silent and snug:
Naught passes between us
   But a brown jug –
     Sometimes!

And sometimes a tear
   Will rise in each eye,
Seeing the two old friends
   So merrily –
     So merrily!

And ere to bed
   Go we, go we,
Down on the ashes
   We kneel on the knee,
     Praying together!

Thus, then, live I
   Till, mid all the gloom,
By heaven! the bold sun
   Is with me in the room
     Shining, shining!

Then the clouds part,
   Swallows soaring between;
The spring is alive,
   And the meadows are green!

I jump up like mad,
Break the old pipe in twain,
And away to the meadows,
   The meadows again!

PO CHU-I

772–846

Translated by Arthur Waley

The Hat given to the Poet by Li Chien

Long ago to a white haired gentleman
You made the present of a black gauze hat.
The gauze hat still sits on my head;
But you already are gone to the Nether Springs.
The thing is old, but still fit to wear;
The man is gone and will never be seen again.
Out on the hill the moon is shining tonight
And the trees on your tomb are swayed by the autumn wind.

A.L. ROWSE

1903–

The White Cat of Trenarren

He was a mighty hunter in his youth
At Polmear all day on the mound, on the pounce
For anything moving, rabbit or bird or mouse –
    My cat and I grow old together.

After a day's hunting he'd come into the house
Delicate ears stuck all with fleas.
At Trenarren I've heard him sigh with pleasure
After a summer's day in the long-grown leas –
    My cat and I grow old together.

When I was a child I played all day
With only a little cat for companion,
At solitary games of my own invention
Under the table or up in the green bay –
    My cat and I grow old together.

When I was a boy I wandered the roads
Up to the downs by gaunt Carn Grey,
Wrapt in a dream at end of day,
All round me the moor, below me the bay –
  My cat and I grow old together.

Now we are too often apart, yet
Turning out of Central Park into the Plaza,
Or walking Michigan Avenue against the lake-wind,
I see a little white shade in the shrubbery
Of far-off Trenarren, never far from my mind –
  My cat and I grow old together.

When I come home from too much travelling,
Cautiously he comes out of his lair to my call,
Receives me at last with a shy reproach
At long absence to him incomprehensible –
  My cat and I grow old together.

Incapable of much or long resentment,
He scratches at my door to be let out
In early morning in the ash moonlight,
Or red dawn breaking through Mother Bond's spinney –
  My cat and I grow old together.

No more frisking as of old,
Or chasing his shadow over the lawn,
But a dignified old person, tickling
His nose against twig or flower in the border,
Until evening falls and bed-time's in order,
Unable to keep eyes open any longer
He waits for me to carry him upstairs
To nestle all night snug at foot of bed –
  My cat and I grow old together.

Careful of his licked and polished appearance,
Ears like shell-whorls pink and transparent,
White plume waving proudly over the paths
Against a background of sea and blue hydrangeas –
  My cat and I grow old together.

EDMUND BLUNDEN

1896–1974

Almswomen

At Quincey's moat the squandering village ends,
And there in the Almshouse dwell the dearest friends
Of all the village, two old dames that cling
As close as any trueloves in the spring.
Long, long ago they passed three-score and ten,
And in this doll's-house lived together then;
All things they have in common being so poor,
And their one fear, Death's shadow at the door.
Each sundown makes them mournful, each sunrise
Brings back the brightness in their failing eyes.

How happy go the rich fair-weather days
When on the roadside folk stare in amaze
At such a honeycomb of fruit and flowers
As mellows round their threshold; what long hours
They gloat upon their steepling hollyhocks,
Bee's balsam, feathery southernwood and stocks,
Fiery dragon's-mouths, great mallow leaves
For salves, and lemon-plants in bushy sheaves,
Shagged Esau's-hands with five green finger-tips.
Such sweet old names are ever on their lips.

As pleased as little children where these grow
In cobbled pattens and worn gowns they go,
Proud of their wisdom when on gooseberry shoots
They stuck egg shells to fright from coming fruits
The brisk-billed rascals; scanning still to see
Their neighbour owls saunter from tree to tree,
Or in the hushing half-light mouse the lane
Long-winged and lordly. But when these hours wane

Indoors they ponder, scared by the harsh storm
Whose pelting saracens on the window swarm,
And listen for the mail to clatter past
And church clock's deep bay withering on the blast;
They feed the fire that flings its freakish light
On pictured kings and queens grotesquely bright,
Platters and pitchers, faded calendars
And graceful hourglass trim with lavenders.

Many a time they kiss and cry and pray
That both be summoned in the selfsame day,
And wiseman linnet tinkling in his cage
End too with them the friendship of old age,
And all together leave their treasured room
Some bell-like evening when the May's in bloom.

YUAN MEI

1792

Translated by R. Kotewell and Norman L. Smith

From Hangehow visiting Su-Sung, P'i-ling, and Chng-k'on, and staying the Night with friends on the way

Seventy-seven, such an old fellow!
In three years I get one look at the West Lake rains;
Back I come, place after place, for a short visit,
Troubling family after family to cook me chicken and millet.
My friends, forbear to ask me the date of my next coming,
For this is an uncertain thing not for my ordering;
I keep saying I will never return and then returning,
And it is shameful to keep cheating folk like this.

HENRY VAUGHAN

1622–1695

Friends Departed

They are all gone into the world of light!
    And I alone sit ling'ring here;
Their very memory is fair and bright,
    And my sad thoughts doth clear.

It glows and glitters in my cloudy breast
    Like stars upon some gloomy grove,
Or those faint beams in which this hill is drest
    After the sun's remove.

I see them walking in an air of glory,
    Whose light doth trample on my days;
My days which are at best but dull and hoary,
    Mere glimmering and decays.

O holy Hope! and high Humility!
    High as the heavens above!
These are your walks, and you have show'd them me,
    To kindle my cold love.

Dear, beauteous Death! the jewel of the Just,
    Shining nowhere, but in the dark
What mysteries do lie beyond thy dust,
    Could man outlook that mark!

He that hath found some fledged bird's nest may know
    At first sight, if the bird be flown;
But what fair well or grove he sings in now,
    That is to him unknown.

And yet as Angels in some brighter dreams
    Call to the soul, when man doth sleep;
So some strange thoughts transcend our wonted themes,
    And into glory peep.

If a star were confined into a tomb
   Her captive flames must needs burn there;
But when the hand that lock'd her up gives room,
   She'll shine through all the sphere.

O Father of eternal life, and all
   Created spirits under Thee!
Resume thy spirit from this world of thrall
   Into true liberty.

Either disperse these mists, which blot and fill
   My perspective still as they pass,
Or else remove me hence unto that hill,
   Where I shall need no glass.

Old loves

FRANCES CORNFORD

1886–1960

All Souls' Night

My love came back to me
Under the November tree
Shelterless and dim.
He put his hand upon my shoulder,
He did not think me strange or older,
Nor I, him.

CHARLOTTE MEW

1869–1928

A Quoi Bon Dire

Seventeen years ago you said
  Something that sounded like Goodbye;
  And everybody thinks that you are dead,
    But I.

So I, as I grow stiff and cold
  To this and that say Goodbye too;
  And everybody sees that I am old
    But you.

  And one fine morning in a sunny lane
Some boy and girl will meet and kiss and swear
  That nobody can love their way again
    While over there
You will have smiled, I shall have tossed your hair.

W.B. YEATS
1865–1939

The Folly of being Comforted

One that is ever kind said yesterday:
'Your well-beloved's hair has threads of grey,
And little shadows come about her eyes;
Time can but make it easier to be wise
Though now it seems impossible, and so
All that you need is patience.'
                Heart cries, 'No,
I have not a crumb of comfort, not a grain.
Time can but make her beauty over again:
Because of that great nobleness of hers
The fire that stirs about her, when she stirs,
Burns but the more brightly. O she had not these ways
When all the wild summer was in her gaze.'

O heart! O heart! if she'd but turn her head,
You'd know the folly of being comforted.

DANTE GABRIEL ROSSETTI
1828–1882

Alas, so Long!

Ah! dear one, we were young so long,
   It seemed that youth would never go,
For skies and trees were ever in song
   And water in singing flow
In the days we never again shall know,
      Alas, so long!
    Ah! then was it all Spring weather?
    Nay, but we were young and together.

Ah! dear one, I've been old so long,
   It seems that age is loth to part,
Though days and years have never a song,
   And oh! have they still the art
That warmed the pulses of heart to heart?
      Alas, so long!
     Ah! then was it all Spring weather?
     Nay, but we were young and together.

Ah! dear one, you've been dead so long, –
   How long until we meet again,
Where hours may never lose their song
   Nor flowers forget the rain
In glad moonlight that shall never wane?
      Alas, so long!
     Ah! shall it be then Spring weather,
     And ah! shall we be young together?

THOMAS HARDY

1840–1928

She to Him

When you shall see me in the toils of Time,
My lauded beauties carried off from me,
My eyes no longer stars as in their prime,
My name forgot of Maiden Fair and Free;

When, in your being, heart concedes to mind,
And judgement, though you scarce its process know,
Recalls the excellencies I once enshrined,
And you are irked that they have withered so;

Remembering mine the loss is, not the blame,
That Sportsman Time but rears his brood to kill,
Knowing me in my soul the very same –
One who would die to spare you touch of ill! –
Will you not grant to old affection's claim
The hand of friendship down Life's sunless hill?

ROBERT HERRICK

1591–1674

On Himself

Young I was, but now am old,
But I am not yet grown cold;
I can play, and I can twine
'Bout a virgin like a vine;
In her lap too I can lie
Melting, and in fancy die:
And return to life, if she
Claps my cheek, or kisseth me;
Thus, and thus it now appears
That our love outlasts our years.

HENRY MARKHAM

1902–

Old Age

There's love still in my heart and in my mind:
The lusting love of youth is left behind.

The tree has reached its old protecting phase,
And underneath the sheep may safely graze.

JOHN BETJEMAN

1906–84

Late-flowering Lust

My head is bald, my breath is bad,
　　Unshaven is my chin,
I have not now the joys I had
　　When I was young in sin.

I run my fingers down your dress
  With brandy-certain aim
And you respond to my caress
  And maybe feel the same.

But I've a picture of my own
  On this reunion night,
Wherein two skeletons are shewn
  To hold each other tight;

Dark sockets look on emptiness
  Which once were loving-eyed,
The mouth that opens for a kiss
  Has got no tongue inside.

I cling to you inflamed with fear
  As now you cling to me,
I feel how frail you are my dear
  And wonder what will be –

A week? or twenty years remain?
  And then – what kind of death?
A losing fight with frightful pain
  Or a gasping fight for breath?

Too long we let our bodies cling,
  We cannot hide disgust
At all the thoughts that in us spring
  From this late-flowering lust.

THOMAS LOVE PEACOCK

1785–1866

Love and Age

I play'd with you mid cowslips blowing,
  When I was six and you were four;
When garlands weaving, flower-balls throwing,
  Were pleasures soon to please no more.

Through groves and meads, through grass and heather,
  With little playmates, to and fro
We wander'd hand in hand together;
  But that was sixty years ago.

You grew a lovely roseate maiden,
  And still our early love was strong;
Still with no care our days were laden,
  They glided joyously along;
And I did love you very dearly,
  How dearly words want power to show;
I thought your heart was touched as nearly;
  But that was fifty years ago.

Then other lovers came around you,
  Your beauty grew from year to year,
And many a splendid circle found you
  The centre of its glittering sphere.
I saw you then first vows forsaking,
  On rank and wealth your hand bestow;
O, then I thought my heart was breaking! –
  But that was forty years ago.

And I lived on to wed another:
  No cause she gave me to repine;
And when I heard you were a mother,
  I did not wish the children mine.
My own young flock, in fair progression,
  Made up a pleasant Christmas row;
My joy in them was past expression;
  But that was thirty years ago.

You grew a matron plump and comely,
  You dwelt in fashion's brightest blaze;
My earthly lot was far more homely;
  But I too had my festal days.
No merrier eyes have ever glisten'd
  Around the hearth-stone's wintry glow,
Than when my youngest child was christened;
  But that was twenty years ago.

Time pass'd. My eldest girl was married,
  And I am now a grandsire gray;
One pet of four years old I've carried
  Among the wild-flower'd meads to play.
In our old fields of childish pleasure,
  Where now, as then, the cowslips blow,
She fills her basket's ample measure;
  And that is not ten years ago.

But though first love's impassion'd blindness
  Has pass'd away in colder light,
I still have thought of you with kindness,
  And shall do, till our last good-night.
The ever-rolling silent hours
  Will bring a time we shall not know,
When our young days of gathering flowers
  Will be an hundred years ago.

W.B. YEATS

1865–1939

From *Quarrel in Old Age*

Where had her sweetness gone?
What fanatics invent
In this blind bitter town,
Fantasy or incident
Not worth thinking of,
Put her in a rage.
I had forgiven enough
That had forgiven old age.

ERNEST DOWSON

1867–1900

In Tempore Senectutis

When I am old,
  And sadly steal apart,

Into the dark and cold,
  Friend of my heart!
Remember, if you can,
Not him who lingers, but that other man,
Who loved and sang, and had a beating heart, –
  When I am old!

When I am old,
  And all love's ancient fire
Be tremulous and cold;
  My soul's desire!
Remember, if you may,
Nothing of you and me but yesterday,
When heart on heart we bid the years conspire
  To make us old.

When I am old,
  And every star above
Be pitiless and cold:
  My life's one love!
Forbid me not to go:
Remember naught of us but long ago,
And not at last how love and pity strove
  When I grow old!

ROBERT HERRICK

1591–1674

Crutches

Thou seest me Lucia this year droop,
Three Zodiacs fill'd more I shall stoop;
Let crutches then provided be
To shore up my debility.
Then while thou laugh'st; I'll, sighing, cry,
A Ruin underpropped am I;
Don will I then my Bedesman's gown,
And when so feeble I am grown,

As my weak shoulders cannot bear
The burden of a Grasshopper;
Yet with the bunch of aged sires,
When I and they keep termly fires;
With my weak voice I'll sing, or say
Some Odes I made of Lucia:
Then will I heave my withered hand
To Jove the Mighty for to stand
Thy faithful friend, and to pour down
Upon thee many a Benison.

W.B. YEATS

1865–1939

After long Silence

Speech after long silence; it is right,
All other lovers being estranged or dead,
Unfriendly lamplight hid under its shade,
The curtains drawn upon unfriendly night,
That we descant and yet again descant
Upon the supreme theme of Art and Song:
Bodily decrepitude is wisdom; young
We loved each other and were ignorant.

R.S. THOMAS

1913–

Seventieth Birthday

Made of tissue and H_2O,
And activated by cells
firing – Ah, heart, the legend
of your person! Did I invent
it, or is it in being still?

In the competition with other
women your victory is assured.
It is time, as Yeats said, is
the caterpillar in the cheek's rose,
the untiring witherer of your petals.

You are drifting away from
me on the whitening current of your hair.
I lean far out from the bone's bough,
knowing the hand I extend
can save nothing of you but your love.

ROBERT HERRICK

1591–1674

Age unfit for Love

Maidens tell me I am old;
Let me in my Glass behold
Whether smooth or not I be,
Or if hair remains to me.
Well, or be't or be't not so,
This for certainty I know;
Ill befits old men to play,
When that Death bids come away.

W.B. YEATS

1865–1939

The Scholars

Bald heads forgetful of their sins,
Old, learned, respectable bald heads
Edit and annotate the lines
That young men, tossing on their beds,
Rhymed out in love's despair
To flatter beauty's ignorant ear.

110

All shuffle there; all cough in ink;
All wear the carpet with their shoes;
All think what other people think;
All know the man their neighbour knows.
Lord, what would they say
Did their Catullus walk their way?

WILLIAM SHAKESPEARE

1564–1616

Sonnet LXXIII

That time of year thou mayst in me behold
When yellow leaves, or none, or few, do hang
Upon those boughs which shake against the cold –
Bare ruin'd choirs, where late the sweet birds sang.
In me thou see'st the twilight of such day
As after sunset fadeth in the west;
Which, by and by black night doth take away,
Death's second self, that seals up all in rest.
In me thou see'st the glowing of such fire,
That on the ashes of his youth doth lie,
As the death-bed whereon it must expire,
Consum'd with that which it was nourish'd by.
 This thou perceiv'st, which makes thy love more strong,
 To love that well which thou must leave ere long.

W.B. YEATS

1865–1939

When you are old

When you are old and grey and full of sleep,
And nodding by the fire, take down this book,
And slowly read, and dream of the soft look
Your eyes had once, and of their shadows deep;

111

How many loved your moments of glad grace,
And loved your beauty with love false or true,
But one man loved the pilgrim soul in you,
And loved the sorrows of your changing face;

And bending down beside the glowing bars,
Murmur, a little sadly, how Love fled
And paced upon the mountains overhead
And hid his face amid a crowd of stars.

PIERRE DE RONSARD

1524–1585

Sonnet

Quand vous serez bien vieille, au soir, à la chandelle,
Assise auprès du feu, devidant et filant,
Direz, chantant mes vers, en vous esmerveillant:
Ronsard me célébroit du temps que j'estois belle.

Lors vous n'aurez servante oyant telle nouvelle,
Desja sous le labeur à demy sommeillant,
Qui au bruit de Ronsard ne s'aille resveillant,
Bénissant vostre nom de louange immortelle.

Je seray sous la terre, et, fantaumi sans os,
Par les ombres hyrteux je prendray mon repos;
Vous serez au fouyer une vieille accroupie,

Regrettant mon amour et vostre fier desdain.
Vivez, si m'en croyez, n'attendez à demain;
Cueillez dès aujourd'huy les roses de la vie.

This French sonnet is included because of its obvious connections with the previous poem by Yeats. As is customary with Ronsard's poems I have printed it in the original spelling.

Pains and indignities

THOMAS HARDY

1840–1928

The Superseded

As newer comers crowd the fore,
    We drop behind.
– We who have laboured long and sore
    Times out of mind,
And keen are yet, must not regret
    To drop behind.

Yet there are some of us who grieve
    To go behind;
Staunch, strenuous souls who scarce believe
    Their fires declined,
And know none spares, remembers, cares
    Who go behind.

'Tis not that we have unforetold
    The drop behind;
We feel the new must oust the old
    In every kind;
But yet we think, must we, must *we*,
    Too, drop behind?

MATTHEW ARNOLD

1822–1888

Growing Old

What is it to grow old?
Is it to lose the glory of the form,
The lustre of the eye?

115

Is it for beauty to forgo her wreath?
Yes, but not this alone.

Is it to feel our strength –
Not our bloom only, but our strength – decay?
Is it to feel each limb
Grow stiffer, every function less exact,
And nerve more weakly strung?

Yes, this, and more! but not,
Ah, 'tis not what in youth we dream'd 'twould be!
'Tis not to have our life
Mellow'd and soften'd as with sunset glow,
A golden day's decline!

'Tis not to see the world
As from a height, with rapt prophetic eyes,
And heart profoundly stirr'd;
And weep, and feel the fullness of the past,
The years that are no more!

It is to spend long days
And not once feel that we were ever young.
It is to add, immured
In the hot prison of the present, month
To month with weary pain.

It is to suffer this,
And feel but half, and feebly, what we feel.
Deep in our hidden heart
Festers the dull remembrance of a change,
But no emotion – none.

It is – last stage of all –
When we are frozen up within, and quite
The phantom of ourselves,
To hear the world applaud the hollow ghost
Which blamed the living man.

WILLIAM SHAKESPEARE

1564–1616

From *Measure for Measure, Act III Scene 1*

. . . when thou art old and rich,
Thou hast neither heat, affection, limb, nor beauty,
To make thy riches pleasant. What's yet in this,
That bears the name of life? Yet in this life
Lie hid more thousand deaths: yet death we fear,
That makes these odds all even.

W.B. YEATS

1865–1939

Why Should not Old Men be Mad?

Why should not old men be mad?
Some have known a likely lad
That had a sound fly-fisher's wrist
Turn to a drunken journalist;
A girl that knew all Dante once
Live to bear children to a dunce;
A Helen of social welfare dream,
Climb on a wagonette to scream.
Some think it a matter of course that chance
Should starve good men and bad advance,
That if their neighbours figured plain,
As though upon a lighted screen,
No single story would they find
Of an unbroken happy mind,
A finish worthy of the start.
Young men know nothing of this sort,
Observant old men know it well;
And when they know what old books tell,
And that no better can be had,
Know why an old man should be mad.

117

THOMAS HARDY

1840–1928

I Look into my Glass

I look into my glass,
And see my wasting skin,
and say, 'Would God it came to pass
My heart had shrunk so thin!'

For then, I, undistrest
By hearts grown cold to me,
Could lonely wait my endless rest
With equanimity.

But Time, to make me grieve,
Part steals, lets part abide;
And shakes this fragile frame at eve
With throbbings of noontide.

WILLIAM SHAKESPEARE

1564–1616

From *As You Like It*, Act II, Scene 7

The sixth age shifts
Into the lean and slipper'd pantaloon,
With spectacles on nose and pouch on side,
His youthful hose well sav'd a world too wide
For his shrunk shank; and his big manly voice
Turning again toward childish treble, pipes
And whistles in his sound. Last scene of all,
That ends this strange eventful history,
Is second childishness and mere oblivion,
Sans teeth, sans eyes, sans taste, sans everything.

PHILIP LARKIN

1922–1983

The Old Fools

What do they think has happened, the old fools,
To make them like this? Do they somehow suppose
It's more grown-up when your mouth hangs open and drools,
And you keep on pissing yourself, and can't remember
Who called this morning? Or that, if they only chose,
They could alter things back to when they danced all night,
Or went to their wedding, or sloped arms some September?
Or do they fancy there's really been no change,
And they've always behaved as if they were crippled or tight,
Or sat through days of thin, continuous dreaming
Watching light move? If they don't (and they can't) it's strange;
     Why aren't they screaming?

At death, you break up: the bits that were you
Start speeding away from each other for ever
With no one to see. It's only oblivion, true:
We had it before, but then it was going to end,
And was all the time merging with a unique endeavour
To bring to bloom the million-petalled flower
Of being here. Next time you can't pretend
There'll be anything else. And these are the first signs:
Not knowing how, not hearing who, the power
Of choosing gone. Their looks show that they're for it:
Ash hair, toad hands, prune faces dried into lines –
     How can they ignore it?

Perhaps being old is having lighted rooms
Inside your head, and people in them, acting.
People you know, yet can't quite name; each looms
Like a deep loss restored, from known doors turning,
Setting down a lamp, smiling from a stair, extracting
A known book from the shelves, or sometimes only
The rooms themselves, chairs and a fire burning,

The blown bush at the window, or the sun's
Faint friendliness on the wall some lonely
Rain-ceased midsummer evening. That is where they live:
Not here and now, but where all happened once.
          That is why they give

An air of baffled absence, trying to be there
Yet being here. For the rooms grow farther, leaving
Incompetent cold, the constant wear and tear
Of taken breath, and then crouching below
Extinction's alp, the old fools, never perceiving
How near it is. This must be what keeps them quiet:
The peak that stays in view wherever we go
For them is rising ground. Can they never tell
What is dragging them back, and how it will end? Not at night?
Not when the strangers come? Never, throughout
The whole hideous inverted childhood? Well,
          We shall find out.

PHILIP LARKIN

1922–1983

Heads in the Women's Ward

On pillow after pillow lies
The wild white hair and staring eyes;
Jaws stand open; necks are stretched
With every tendon sharply sketched;
A bearded mouth talks silently
To someone no one else can see.

Sixty years ago they smiled
At lover, husband, first-born child.

Smiles are for youth. For old age come
Death's terror and delirium.

120

IAIN CRICHTON SMITH
1928–

Old Woman

And she, being old, fed from a mashed plate
as an old mare might droop across a fence
to the dull pastures of its ignorance.
Her husband held her upright while he prayed

to God who is all-forgiving to send down
some angel somewhere who might land perhaps
in his foreign wings among the gradual crops.
She munched, half dead, blindly searching the spoon.

Outside, the grass was raging. There I sat
imprisoned in my pity and my shame
that men and women having suffered time
should sit in such a place, in such a state

and wished to be away, yes, to be far away
with athletes, heroes, Greeks or Roman men
who pushed their bitter spears into a vein
and would not spend an hour with such decay,

'Pray God,' he said, 'we ask you, God,' he said.
The bowed back was quiet. I saw the teeth
tighten their grip around a delicate death.
And nothing moved within the knotted head

but only a few poor veins as one might see
vague wishless seaweed floating on a tide
of all the salty waters where had died
too many waves to mark two more or three.

W.H. AUDEN
1907–1973

Old People's Home

All are limitory, but each has her own
nuance of damage. The elite can dress and decent themselves,
   are ambulant with a single stick, adroit
to read a book all through, or play the slow movement of
   easy sonatas. (Yet, perhaps their very
carnal freedom is their spirit's bane: intelligent
   of what has happened, and why, they are obnoxious
to a glum beyond tears.) Then comes those on wheels, the average
   majority, who endure T.V. and, led by
lenient therapists, do community-singing, then
   the loners, muttering in Limbo, and last
the terminally incompetent, as improvident,
   unspeakable, impeccable as the plants
they parody. (Plants may sweat profusely but never
   sully themselves.) One tie, though, unites them: all
appeared when the world, though much was awry there, was more
   spacious, more comely to look at, its Old Ones
with an audience and secular station. Then a child,
   in dismay with Mamma, could refuge with Gran
To be revalued and told a story, As of now,
   we all know what to expect, but their generation
is the first to fade like this, not at home but assigned
   to a numbered frequent ward, stowed out of conscience
as unpopular luggage.
            As I ride the subway
to spend half-an-hour with one, I revisage
who she was in the pomp and sumpture of her hey-day,
   when week-end visits were a presumptive joy,
not a good work. Am I cold to wish for a speedy
   painless dormition, pray, as I know she prays,
that God or Nature will abrupt her earthly function?

JONATHAN SWIFT

1667–1745

From *Verses on the Death of Dean Swift*

The time is not remote when I
Must by the course of nature die:
When I foresee my special friends
Will try to find their private ends:
Though it is hardly understood
Which way my death can do them good;
Yet, thus methinks I hear 'em speak:
'See how the Dean begins to break,
Poor gentleman, he droops apace,
You plainly find it in his face;
That old vertigo in his head
Will never leave him till he's dead:
Besides, his memory decays,
He recollects not what he says,
He cannot call his friends to mind,
Forgets the place where last he dined,
Plies you with stories o'er and o'er –
He told them fifty times before.
How does he fancy we can sit
To hear his out-of-fashioned wit?
But he takes up with younger folks,
Who for his wine will bear his jokes,
Faith, he must make his stories shorter,
Or change his comrades once a quarter;
In half the time he talks them round,
There must another set be found.

For poetry, he's past his prime,
He takes an hour to find a rhyme;
His fire is out, his wit decayed,
His fancy sunk, his muse a jade.
I'd have him throw away his pen,
But there's no talking to some men.'

And then their tenderness appears,
By adding largely to my years:
'He's older than he would be reckoned,
And well remembers Charles the Second.'

'He hardly drinks a pint of wine,
And that, I doubt, is no good sign.
His stomach too begins to fail:
Last year we thought him strong and hale,
But now he's quite another thing;
I wish he may hold out till spring.'

Then hug themselves and reason thus:
'It is not yet so bad with us.'

PHILIP LARKIN

1922–1983

The Winter Palace

Most people know more as they grow older;
I give all that the cold shoulder.

I spent my second quarter-century
Losing what I learnt at university

And refusing to take in what had happened since.
Now I know none of the names in the public prints,

And am starting to give offence by forgetting faces
And swearing I've never been in certain places.

It will be worth it, if in the end I manage
To blank out whatever it is that is doing the damage,

Then there will be nothing I know.
My mind will fold into itself, like fields, like snow.

THOMAS HARDY

1840–1928

In a Former Resort after Many Years

Do I know these, slack-shaped and wan,
Whose substance, one time fresh and furrowless,
Is now a rag drawn over a skeleton,
    As in El Greco's canvases? —
Whose cheeks have slipped down, lips become indrawn,
    And statures shrunk to dwarfishness?

Do they know me, whose former mind
Was like an open mind where no foot falls,
But now is as a gallery portrait-lined,
    And scored with necrologic scrawls,
Where feeble voices rise, once full-defined,
    From underground in curious calls?

WILLIAM SHAKESPEARE

1564–1616

From *Macbeth, Act V Scene 3*

I have lived long enough: my way of life
Is fall'n into the sear, the yellow leaf;
And that which should accompany old age,
As honour, love, obedience, troops of friends,
I must not look to have, but, in their stead,
Curses, not loud but deep, mouth-honour, breath,
Which the poor heart would fain deny, but dare not.

125

W.B. YEATS

1865–1939

The Spur

You think it horrible that lust and rage
Should dance attendance upon my old age;
They were not such a plague when I was young;
What else have I to spur me into song?

PO CHU-I

772–846

Translated by Arthur Waley

Poem in Depression, at Wei Village

I hug my pillow and do not speak a word;
In my empty room no sound stirs.
Who knows that, all day a-bed,
I am not ill, and am not even asleep?

Turned to jade are the boy's rosy cheeks;
To his sick temples the frost of winter clings –
Do not wonder that my body sinks to decay;
Though my limbs are old, my heart is older yet.

PHILIP LARKIN

1922–1983

Age

My age fallen away like white swaddling
Floats in the middle distance, becomes
An inhabited cloud. I bend closer, discern
A lighted tenement scuttling with voices.

126

O you tall game I tired myself with joining!
Now I wade through you like knee-level weeds,

And they attend me, dear translucent bergs:
Silence and space. By now so much has flown
from the nest here of my head that I needs must turn
To know what prints I leave, whether of feet,
Or spoor of pads, or a bird's adept splay.

GEORGE CRABBE

1754–1832

From *The Borough*
Old Age in the Workhouse

Your plan I love not; – with a number you
Have placed your poor, your pitiable few;
There, in one house, throughout their lives to be,
The pauper-palace which they hate to see;
That giant-building, that high-bounding wall,
Those bare-worn walks, that lofty thund'ring hall!
That large loud clock, which tolls each dreaded hour,
Those gates and locks, and all those signs of power:
It is a prison, with a milder name,
Which few inhabit without dread or shame. . .

Then too I own, it grieves me to behold
Those ever virtuous, helpless now and old,
By all for care and industry approved,
For truth respected, and for temper loved;
And who, by sickness and misfortune tried,
Gave want its worth, and poverty its pride:
I own it grieves me to behold them sent
From their old home; 'tis pain, 'tis punishment,
To leave each scene familiar, every face,
For a new people and a stranger race;
For those who, sunk in sloth and dead to shame
From scenes of guilt with daring spirits came;

Men, just and guileless, at such manners start,
And bless their God that time has fenced their heart,
Confirmed their virtue, and expell'd the fear
Of vice in minds so simple and sincere.

Here the good pauper. losing all the praise
By worthy deeds acquired in better days,
Breathes a few months, then to his chamber led,
Expires, while strangers chatter round his bed.
The grateful hunter, when his horse is old,
Wills not the useless favourite to be sold;
He knows his former worth, and gives him place
In some fair pasture, till he runs his race:
But has the labourer, has the seaman done
Less worthy service, though not dealt to one?
Shall we not then contribute to their ease,
In their old haunts, where ancient objects please?
That, till their sight shall fail them, they may trace
The well-known prospect and the long-loved face. . .

What venerable ruin man appears!
How worthy pity, love, respect, and grief –
He claims protection – he compels relief; –
And shall we send him from our view, to brave
The storms abroad, whom we at home might save,
And let a stranger dig our ancient brother's grave?
No! – we will shield him from the storm he fears,
And when he falls, embalm him with our tears.

WILLIAM WORDSWORTH

1770–1850

From *The Old Cumberland Beggar*

– Then let him pass, a blessing on his head!
And, long as he can wander, let him breathe
The freshness of the valleys; let his blood
Struggle with frosty air and winter snows;

And let the chartered wind that sweeps the heath
Beat his grey locks against his withered face.
Reverence the hope whose vital anxiousness
Gives the last human interest to his heart.
May never HOUSE, misnamed of INDUSTRY,
Make him a captive! – for that pent-up din,
Those life-consuming sounds that clog the air,
Be his the natural silence of old age!
Let him be free of mountain solitudes;
And have around him, whether heard or not,
The pleasant melody of woodland birds.
Few are his pleasures: if his eyes have now
Been doomed so long to settle upon earth
That not without some effort they behold
The countenance of the horizontal sun,
Rising and setting, let the light at least
Find a free entrance to their languid orbs,
And let him, *where* and *when* he will, sit down
Beneath the trees, or on a grassy bank
Of highway side, and with the little birds
Share his chance-gathered meal; and, finally,
As in the eye of Nature he has lived,
So in the eye of Nature let him die!

PSALM NINETY

(Book of Common Prayer version)

Verses 8–12

Thou hast set our misdeeds before thee: and
our secret sins in the light of thy countenance.

For when thou art angry all our days are gone:
we bring our years to an end, as it were a tale
that is told.

The days of our age are threescore years and ten;
and though men be so strong that they come to

fourscore years: yet is their strength then but labour and sorrow; so soon passeth it away, and we are gone.

But who regardeth the power of thy wrath: for even thereafter as a man feareth, so is thy displeasure.

So teach us to number our days: that we may apply our hearts unto wisdom.

Comfort and joy

GEORGE HERBERT

1593–1633

From *The Flower*

And now in age I bud again,
After so many deaths I live and write;
   I once more smell the dew and rain,
And relish versing: O my only light
      It cannot be
      That I am he
On whom thy tempests fell all night.

PO CHU'I

772–846

Translated by Arthur Waley

Ease

(Written when he was 72)

Lined coat, warm cap and easy felt slippers,
In the little tower, at the low window, sitting
      over the sunken brazier.
Body at rest, heart at peace; no need to rise early.
I wonder if the courtiers at the Western
      Capital know of these things or not?

JAMES LEIGH HUNT

1784–1859

Rondeau

Jenny kiss'd me when we met,
  Jumping from the chair she sat in;
Time, you thief, who love to get
  Sweets into your list, put that in!

Say I'm weary, say I'm sad,
  Say that health and wealth have missed me.
Say I'm growing old, but add,
  Jenny kiss'd me.

W.B. YEATS

1865–1939

A Prayer for Old Age

God guard me from those thoughts men think
In the mind alone;
He that sings a lasting song
Thinks in a marrow-bone;

From all that makes a wise old man
That can be praised of all;
O what am I that I should not seem
For the song's sake a fool?

I pray – for fashion's word is out
And prayer comes round again –
That I may seem, though I die old,
A foolish, passionate man.

D.H. LAWRENCE

1885–1930

Beautiful Old Age

It ought to be lovely to be old
to be full of the peace that comes of experience
and wrinkled ripe fulfilment.

The wrinkled smile of completeness that follows a life
Lived undaunted and unsoured with accepted lies.
If people lived without accepting lies
they would ripen like apples, and be scented like pippins
in their old age.

Soothing, old people should be, like apples
when one is tired of love,
Fragrant like yellowing leaves, and dim with the soft
stillness and satisfaction of autumn.

And a girl should say:
It must be wonderful to live and grow old.
Look at my mother, how rich and still she is!

And a young man should think: By Jove
my father has faced all weathers, but it's been a life!

ROBERT HERRICK

1591–1674

The Plaudits, or
End of Life

If after rude and boisterous seas,
My wearied Pinnace here finds ease:
If so it be I've gained the shore
With safety of a faithful Oar:
If having run my Barque on ground,
Ye see the aged vessel crowned:
What's to be done? but on the Sands
Ye dance, and sing, and now clap hands.
The first Act's doubtful (but we say)
It is the last commends the Play.

135

ALFRED, LORD TENNYSON
1809–1892

Ulysses

It little profits that an idle king,
By this still hearth, among these barren crags,
Match'd with an aged wife, I mete and dole
Unequal laws unto a savage race,
That hoard, and sleep, and feed, and know not me.
I cannot rest from travel: I will drink
Life to the lees: all time I have enjoy'd
Greatly, have suffer'd greatly, both with those
That loved me, and alone; on shore, and when
Thro' scudding drifts the rainy Hyades
Vext the dim sea: I am become a name;
For always roaming with a hungry heart,
Much have I seen and known; cities and men
And manners, climates, councils, governments,
Myself not least, but honour'd of them all;
And drunk delight of battle with my peers,
Far on the ringing plains of windy Troy.
I am a part of all that I have met;
Yet all experience is an arch wherethro'
Gleams that untravelled world, whose margin fades
For ever and for ever when I move.
How dull it is to pause, to make an end,
To rust unburnish'd, not to shine in use! . . .

There lies the port; the vessel puffs her sail;
There gloom the dark broad seas. My mariners,
Souls that have toil'd, and wrought, and thought with me —
That ever with a frolic welcome took
The thunder and the sunshine, and opposed
Free hearts, free foreheads — you and I are old;
Old age hath yet his honour and his toil;
Death closes all: but something ere the end,
Some work of noble note, may yet be done,

Not unbecoming men that strove with Gods.
The lights begin to twinkle from the rocks;
The long day wanes: the slow moon climbs: the deep
Moans round with many voices. Come, my friends,
'Tis not too late to seek a newer world.
Push off, and sitting well in order smite
The sounding furrows; for my purpose holds
To sail beyond the sunset, and the baths
Of all the western stars, until I die.
It may be that the gulfs will wash us down:
It may be we shall touch the Happy Isles,
And see the great Achilles, whom we knew.
Tho' much is taken, much abides; and tho'
We are not now that strength which in old days
Moved earth and heaven; that which we are, we are;
One equal temper of heroic hearts,
Made weak by time and fate, but strong in will
To strive, to seek, to find, and not to yield.

PO CHU-I

772–846

Translated by Arthur Waley

A Dream of Mountaineering

(written when he was over seventy)

At night, in my dream, I stoutly climbed a mountain,
Going out alone with my staff of holly-wood.
A thousand crags, a hundred hundred valleys –
In my dream-journey none were unexplored
And all the while my feet never grew tired
And my step was as strong as in my young days.
Can it be that when the mind travels backward
The body also returns to its old state?
And can it be, as between body and soul,
That the body may languish, while the soul is still strong?
Soul and body – both are vanities:
Dreaming and waking – both alike unreal.

In the day my feet are palsied and tottering,
In the night my feet go striding over the hills.
As day and night are divided in equal parts —
Between the two, I *get* as much as I *lose*.

OLIVER GOLDSMITH

1728–1774

From *The Deserted Village*

Sweet Auburn, parent of the blissful hour,
Thy glades forlorn confess the tyrant's power,
Here as I take my solitary rounds,
Amidst thy tangling walks and ruin'd grounds,
And, many a year elapsed, return to view
Where once the cottage stood, the hawthorn grew,
Remembrance wakes with all her busy train,
Swells at my breast, and turns the past to pain.
    In all my wanderings round this world of care,
In all my griefs — and God has giv'n my share —
I still had hopes, my latest hours to crown,
Amid these humble bowers to lay me down;
To husband out life's taper at the close,
And keep the flames from wasting by repose;
I still had hopes — for pride attends us still,
Amid the swains to show my book-learn'd skill,
Around my fire an evening group to draw,
And tell of all I felt, and all I saw;
And, as a hare, whom hounds and horn pursue,
Pants to the place from whence at first he flew,
I still had hopes, my long vexations past,
Here to return —and die at home at last.
    O blest retirement! friend to life's decline,
Retreats from care, that never must be mine,
How blest is he who crowns in shades like these
A youth of labour with an age of ease;
Who quits a world where strong temptations try,
And, since 'tis hard to combat, learns to fly!

138

For him no wretches, born to work and weep,
Explore the mine, or tempt the dangerous deep;
No surly porter stands in guilty state,
To spurn imploring famine from the gate;
But on he moves to meet his latter end,
Angels around befriending virtue's friend:
Sinks to the grave with unperceived decay,
While resignation gently slopes the way;
And all his prospects brightening to the last,
His heaven commences ere the world be past.

ALEXANDER POPE

1688–1744

Imitation of Martial, Book 10 Epig. 23

At length my friend (while time, with still career,
Wafts on his gentle wing his eightieth year)
Sees his past days safe out of Fortune's power,
Nor dreads approaching fate's uncertain hour;
Reviews his life, and in the strict survey
Finds not one moment he could wish away,
Pleased with the series of each happy day.
Such, such a man extends his life's short space,
And from the goal again renews the race;
For he lives twice, who can at once employ
The present well, and ev'n the past enjoy.

HENRY NEWBOLT

1862–1938

Felix Antonius. (After Martial)

Today my friend is seventy-five;
  He tells his tale with no regret;
  His brave old eyes are steadfast yet,
His heart the lightest heart alive.

He sees behind him green and wide
   The pathway of his pilgrim years;
   He sees the shore, and dreadless hears
The whisper of the creeping tide.

For out of all his days, not one
   Has passed and left its unlaid ghost
   To seek a light for ever lost,
Or wail a deed for ever done.

So for reward of life-long truth
   He lives again, as good men can,
   Redoubling his allotted span
With memories of a stainless youth.

WILLIAM WORDSWORTH

1770–1850

From *Resolution and Independence*

. . . Now, whether it were by peculiar grace,
A leading from above, a something given,
Yet it befell that, in this lonely place,
When I with these untoward thoughts had striven,
Beside a pool bare to the eye of heaven
I saw a man before me unawares:
The oldest man he seemed that ever wore grey hairs.

As a huge stone is sometimes seen to lie
Couched on the bald top of an eminence;
Wonder to all who do the same espy,
By what means it could thither come, and whence;
So that it seemed a thing endued with sense:
Like a sea-beast crawled forth, that on a shelf
Of rock or sand reposeth, there to sun itself;

Such seemed this Man, not all alive nor dead,
Nor all asleep in his extreme old age;
His body was bent double, feet and head
Coming together in life's pilgrimage;
As if some dire constraint of pain, or rage
Of sickness felt by him in times long past,
A more than human weight upon his frame had cast.

Himself he propped, limbs, body, and pale face,
Upon a long grey staff of shaven wood:
And, still as I drew near with gentle pace,
Upon the margin of that moorish flood
Motionless as a cloud the old Man stood,
That heareth not the loud winds when they call;
And moveth all together, if it move at all.

At length, himself unsettling, he the pond
Stirred with his staff, and fixedly did look
Upon the muddy water, which he conned,
As if he had been reading in a book:
And now a stranger's privilege I took;
And, drawing to his side, to him did say,
'This morning gives us promise of a glorious day.'

A gentle answer did the old Man make,
In courteous speech which forth he slowly drew:
And him with further words I thus bespake,
'What occupation do you here pursue?
This is a lonesome place for one like you.'
Ere he replied, a flash of mild surprise
Broke from the sable orbs of his yet-vivid eyes.

His words came feebly, from a feeble chest,
But each in solemn order followed each,
With something of a lofty utterance drest –
Choice word and measured phrase, above the reach
of ordinary men; a stately speech;
Such as grave Livers do in Scotland use,
Religious men, who give to God and man their dues.

He told, that to these waters he had come
To gather leeches, being old and poor:
Employment hazardous and wearisome!
And he had many hardships to endure:
From pond to pond he roamed, from moor to moor;
Housing, with God's good help, by choice or chance;
And in this way he gained an honest maintenance.

The old Man still stood talking by my side;
But now his voice to me was like a stream
Scarce heard; nor word from word could I divide;
And the whole body of the Man did seem
Like one whom I had met with in a dream;
Or like a man from some far region sent,
To give me human strength, by apt admonishment.

My former thoughts returned: the fear that kills;
And hope that is unwilling to be fed;
Cold, pain, and labour, and all fleshly ills;
And mighty Poets in their misery dead.
Perplexed, and longing to be comforted,
My question eagerly did I renew,
'How is it that you live, and what is it you do?'

He with a smile did then his words repeat;
And said that, gathering leeches, far and wide
He travelled; stirring thus about his feet
The waters of the pools where they abide.
'Once I could meet with them on every side;
But they have dwindled long by slow decay;
Yet still I persevere, and find them where I may'.

While he was talking thus, the lonely place,
The old Man's shape and speech – all troubled me:
In my mind's eye I seemed to see him pace
About the weary moors continually,
Wandering about alone and silently.
While I these thoughts within myself pursued,
He, having made a pause, the same discourse renewed.

And soon with this he other matter blended,
Cheerfully uttered, with demeanour kind,
But stately in the main; and when he ended,
I could have laughed myself to scorn to find
In that decrepit Man so firm a mind.
'God' said I, 'be my help and stay secure;
I'll think of the Leech-gatherer on the lonely moor!'

ROBERT HERRICK

1591–1674

Youth and Age

God on our Youth bestows but little ease;
But on our Age most sweet Indulgences.

ELIZABETH JENNINGS

1926–

Rembrandt's Late Self-Portraits

You are confronted with yourself. Each year
The pouches fill, the skin is uglier.
You give it all unflinchingly. You stare
Into yourself, beyond. Your brush's care
Runs with self-knowledge. Here

Is a humility at one with craft.
There is no arrogance. Pride is apart
From this self-scrutiny. You make light drift
The way you want. Your face is bruised and hurt
But there is still love left.

Love of the art and others. To the last
Experiment went on. You stared beyond
Your age, the times. You also plucked to past
And tempered it. Self-portraits understand
And old age can divest,

With truthful changes, us of fear of death.
Look, a new anguish. There, the bloated nose,
The sadness and the joy. To paint's to breathe,
And all the darknesses are dared. You chose
What each must reckon with.

ROBERT HERRICK

1591–1674

His wish to God

I would to God, that mine old age might have
Before my last, but here a living grave,
Some one poor Alms-house; there to lie, or stir,
Ghost-like, as in my meaner sepulcre;
A little piggin,* and a pipkin† by,
To hold things fitting my necessity;
Which, rightly us'd, both in their time and place,
Might me excite to fore, and after-grace.
Thy Cross, my Christ, fixed 'fore mine eyes should be,
Not to adore that, but to worship Thee.
So, here the remnant of my days I'd spend,
Reading Thy Bible, and my Book; so end.

* A small bowl
† A small earthenware pot

JOHN MASEFIELD

1878–1967

On Growing Old

Be with me, Beauty, for the fire is dying;
My dog and I are old, too old for roving.
Man, whose young passion sets the spindrift flying,
Is soon too lame to march, too cold for loving.

I take the book and gather to the fire,
Turning old yellow leaves; minute by minute
The clock ticks to my heart. A withered wire,
Moves a thin ghost of music in the spinet.
I cannot sail your seas, I cannot wander
Your cornland, nor your hill-land, nor your valleys
Ever again, nor share the battle yonder
Where the young knight the broken squadron rallies.
Only stay quiet while my mind remembers
The beauty of fire from the beauty of embers.

Beauty, have pity! for the strong have power,
The rich their wealth, the beautiful their grace,
Summer of man its sunlight and its flower,
Spring-time of man all April in a face.
Only, as in the jostling in the Strand,
Where the mob thrusts or loiters or is loud,
The beggar with the saucer in his hand
Asks only a penny from the passing crowd,
So, from this glittering world with all its fashion,
Its fire, and play of men, its stir, its march,
Let me have wisdom, Beauty, wisdom and passion,
Bread to the soul, rain where the summers parch,
Give me but these, and, though the darkness close,
Even the night will blossom as the rose.

ELIZABETH JENNINGS

1926–

Old Man

His age draws out behind him to be watched;
It is his shadow you may say. That dark
He paints upon the wall is his past self,
A mark he only leaves when he is still
    And he is still now always,
At ease and watching all his life assemble.

145

And he intends nothing but watching. What
His life has made of him his shadow shows –
Fine graces gone but dignity remaining,
While all he shuffled after is composed
    Into a curve of dark, of silences:
An old man tranquil in his silences.

And we move round him, are his own world turning,
Spinning it seems to him, leaving no shadow
To blaze our trail. We are our actions only:
He is himself, abundant and assured,
    All action thrown away,
And time is slowing where his shadow stands.

ELIZABETH JENNINGS

1926–

Old Woman

So much she caused she cannot now account for
As she stands watching day return, the cool
Walls of the house moving towards the sun.
She puts some flowers in a vase and thinks
    'There is not much I can arrange
In here and now, but flowers are suppliant

As children never were. And love is now
A flicker of memory, my body is
My own entirely. When I lie at night
I gather nothing now into my arms,
    No child or man, and where I live
Is what remains when men and children go.'

Yet she owns more than residue of lives
That she has marked and altered. See how she
Warns time from too much touching her possessions
By keeping flowers fed, by polishing
    Her fine old silver. Gratefully
She sees her own glance printed on grandchildren.

146

Drawing the curtains back and opening windows
Every morning now, she feels her years
Grow less and less. Time puts no burden on
Her now she does not need to measure it.
    It is acceptance she arranges
And her own life she places in the vase.

WILLIAM EMPSON

1906–1984

To
an Old Lady

Ripeness is all; her in her cooling planet
Revere; do not presume to think her wasted.
Project her no projectile, plan nor man it;
Gods cool in turn, by the sun long outlasted.

Our earth alone given no name of god
Gives, too, no hold for such a leap to aid her;
Landing, you break some palace and seem odd;
Bees sting their need, the keeper's queen invader.

No, to your telescope; spy out the land;
Watch while her ritual is still to see,
Still stand her temples emptying in the sand
Whose waves o'erthrow their crumbled tracery;

Still stands uncalled-on her soul's appanage;
Much social detail whose successor fades,
Wit used to run a house and to play Bridge,
And tragic fervour, to dismiss her maids.

Years her precession do not throw from gear.
She reads a compass certain of her pole;
Confident, finds no confines in her sphere,
Whose failing crops are in her sole control.

Stars how much further from me fill my night.
Strange that she too should be inaccessible,
Who shares my sun. He curtains her from sight,
And but in darkness is she visible.

COLIN ELLIS

1895–1969

The Old Ladies

They walked in straitened ways,
 They had not great possessions;
They lived before the days
 When ladies learned professions.

And one was rather mad
 And all were rather trying,
So little life they had,
 So long they spent a-dying.

In spotless white lace caps,
 Just sitting, sitting, sitting,
Their hands upon their laps
 Or occupied with knitting.

And now they all are gone,
 Miss Alice and Miss Ella,
Miss Jane (at ninety-one)
 And poor Miss Arabella.

The house they loved so well
 and always kept so nicely,
Some auctioneer will sell
 'At six o'clock precisely'.

It seemed as though their lives
 Were wasted more than others';
They would have made good wives
 They might have made good mothers.

Yet this was their reward:
    Through ninety years of leisure
Small precious things to guard,
    None else had time to treasure.

Their crystal was their pride,
    Their porcelain a token,
Kept safe until they died
    And handed on unbroken.

SAMUEL JOHNSON

1709–1784

From *On the Death of Mr Robert Levet, A Practiser in Physic*

Well tried through many a varying year,
    See Levet to the grave descend;
Officious,* innocent, sincere,
    Of every friendless name the friend. . .

His virtues walked their narrow round,
    Nor made a pause, nor left a void;
And sure the Eternal Master found
    The single talent well employed.

The busy day, the peaceful night,
    Unfelt, uncounted, glided by;
His frame was firm – his powers were bright,
    Though now his eightieth year was nigh.

Then with no fiery throbbing pain,
    No cold gradations of decay,
Death broke at once the vital chain,
    And freed his soul the nearest way.

* Obliging (obsolete meaning)

149

ANDREW YOUNG

1885–1971

The Blind Man

How often it comes back to me,
The small white cottage looking out to the blue sea
Over the bents bleared with an oily heat,
And seated on the rustic seat
The old, old man with thick
Fingers bunched on his varnished walking stick;
But he looked out on nothing – he was blind,
Blind to all but the sunny wind
Whirling the two jack-tars on their tall pole,
That round and round would roll
In their blue jackets and white trousers;
Whichever way the wind went,
Those wooden sailors were no drowsers,
Though he would sometimes sleep in the hot scent
Of stocks, moss-roses, southern-wood, and sweet-william,
But when he raised a listening finger,
Each bird-note in the silence seemed to linger,
Till to the bird he gave a name,
Wren, chaffinch, robin, tit, he knew their cries,
Though all were nightingales to his blind eyes.

W.B. YEATS

1865–1939

An Acre of Grass

Picture and book remain,
An acre of green grass
For air and exercise,
Now strength of body goes;
Midnight, an old house
Where nothing stirs but a mouse.

My temptation is quiet,
Here at life's end
Neither loose imagination,
Nor the mill of the mind
Consuming its rag and bone,
Can make the truth known.

Grant me an old man's frenzy,
Myself must I remake
Till I am Timon and Lear
Or that William Blake
Who beat upon the wall
Till Truth obeyed his call;

A mind Michael Angelo knew
That can pierce the clouds,
Or inspired by frenzy
Shake the dead in their shrouds;
Forgotten else by mankind,
An old man's eagle mind.

WALTER DE LA MARE

1873–1956

All Gone

'Age takes in pitiless hands
All one loves most away;
Peace, joy, simplicity
Where then their inward stay?

Or so, at least, they say.

'Marvel of noontide light,
Of gradual break of day;
Dreams, visions of the night
Age withers all away!

Yes, that is what they say.

151

'Wonder of winter snow,
Magic of wandering moon,
The starry hosts of heaven –
Come seventy, all are gone.

'Unhappy when alone,
Nowhere at peace to be;
Drowned the old, self-sown eager thoughts
Constantly stirring in thee!'

Extraordinary!
That's what they say to me!

PHILIP LARKIN

1922–1985

Long Sight in Age

They say eyes clear with age,
As dew clarifies air
To sharpen evenings,
As if time put an edge
Round the last shape of things
To show them there;
The many-levelled trees,
The long soft tides of grass
Wrinkling away the gold
Wind-ridden waves – all these,
They say, come back to focus
As we grow old.

MARGARET CROPPER

1886–1980

Old Age

Perhaps I have ended doing, effective doing,
'Si vieillesse pouvait', the bitter screed runs to rust,

Limbs stiffen, energy is not in excess
Of needs that must be met. Perhaps I have done
The best of my work, and must work clumsily now –
But there's one word that rings with curious comfort,
I can watch, and indeed I think I see exquisite things
That never before gave me such haunting joy,
Such pangs of sharp edged pleasure, such surprise.
If I am confined to a mile or two of country
I shall never be starved:
A branch with its trimming of tiny leaves in May,
The gaunt ash holding up her dark grave blossom,
A patch of primroses spreading deliciously
In unexpected places; and when I dare,
For beauty always longs to be matched with daring,
I can look at the sky – Can it always have been like this?
But I have not watched it or found it so rapturous –
Old age is flooded with unexpected delights –
Sprung from the brimming cup of eternity.

JOHN BETJEMAN

1906–84

Felixstowe, or The Last of Her Order

With one consuming roar along the shingle
   The long wave claws and rakes the pebbles down
To where its backwash and the next wave mingle,
   A mounting arch of water weedy-brown
Against the tide the off-shore breezes blow.
Oh wind and water, this is Felixstowe.

In winter when the sea winds chill and shriller
   Than those of summer, all their cold unload
Full on the gimcrack attic of the villa
   Where I am lodging off the Orwell Road,
I put my final shilling in the meter
And only make my loneliness completer.

In eighteen ninety-four when we were founded,
 Counting our Reverend Mother we were six,
Now full of hope we were and prayer-surrounded
 – 'The Little Sisters of the Hanging Pyx'.
We built our orphanage. We ran our school.
Now only I am left to keep the rule.

Here in the gardens of the Spa Pavilion
 Warm in the whisper of a summer sea,
The cushioned scabious, a deep vermilion,
 With white pins stuck in it, looks up at me
A sun-lit kingdom full of butterflies
And so my memory of winter dies.

Across the grass the poplar shades grow longer
 And louder clang the waves along the coast
The band packs up. The evening breeze is stronger
 And all the world goes home to tea and toast.
I hurry past a cakeshop's tempting scones
Bound for the red brick twilight of St John's.

'Thou knowest my down sitting and mine uprising'
 Here where the white light burns with steady glow
Safe from the vain world's silly sympathising,
 Safe with the Love that I was born to know,
Safe from the surging of the lonely sea
My heart finds rest, my heart finds rest in Thee.

KATHERINE CHORLEY

1897–1986

The Hearth

I, too, have lived by a hearth not tended,
 The coals gone cold;
Yet at times unheralded a hand has mended
 The sad embers
And a flicker has turned the bleak Decembers
 Briefly to gold.

W.B. YEATS

1865–1939

From *The Tower*

What shall I do with this absurdity –
O heart, O troubled heart – this caricature,
Decrepit age that has been tied to me
As to a dog's tail?
                Never had I more
Excited, passionate, fantastical
Imagination, nor an ear and eye
That more expected the impossible –
No, not in boyhood when with rod and fly,
Or the humbler worm, I climbed Ben Bulben's back
And had the livelong summer day to spend.
It seems I must bid the Muse go pack,
Choose Plato and Plotinus for a friend
Until imagination, ear and eye,
Can be content with argument and deal
In abstract things; or be derided by
A sort of battered kettle at the heel. . .

Now shall I make my soul,
Compelling it to study
In a learned school
Till the wreck of body,
Slow decay of blood,
Testy delirium
Or dull decrepitude,
Or what worse evil come –
The death of friends, or death
Of every brilliant eye
That made a catch in the breath –
Seem but the clouds of the sky
When the horizon fades;
Or a bird's sleepy cry
Among the deepening shades.

WILLIAM WORDSWORTH

1770–1850

Animal Tranquility
and Decay

The little hedgerow birds
That peck along the road, regard him not.
He travels on, and in his face, his step,
His gait, is one expression: every limb,
His looks and bending figure, all bespeak
A man who does not move with pain but moves
With thought. – He is insensibly subdued
To settled quiet: he is one by whom
All effort seems forgotten; one to whom
Long patience hath such mild composure given
That patience now doth seem a thing of which
He hath no need. He is by nature led
To peace so perfect that the young behold
With envy, what the Old Man hardly feels.

W.B. YEATS

1865–1939

The Coming of Wisdom
with Time

Though leaves are many, the root is one;
Through all the lying days of my youth
I swayed my leaves and flowers in the sun;
Now I may wither into the truth.

PO CHU-I

772–846

Translated by Arthur Waley

Last Poem

They have put my bed beside the unpainted screen;
They have shifted my stove in front of the blue curtain.
I listen to my grandchildren reading me a book;
I watch the servants, heating up my soup.
With rapid pencil I answer the poems of friends,
I feel in my pocket and pull out medicine-money,
When this superintendence of trifling affairs is done
I lie back on my pillows and sleep with my face to the South.

EDMUND WALLER

1606–1687

Old Age

The seas are quiet when the winds give o'er;
So calm are we when passions are no more.
For then we know how vain it was to boast
Of fleeting things, so certain to be lost.
Clouds of affection from our younger eyes
Concealed that emptiness which age descries.

The soul's dark cottage, batter'd and decay'd,
Let in new light through chinks that Time hath made:
Stronger by weakness, wiser men become
As they draw near to their eternal home.
Leaving the old, both worlds at once they view
That stand upon the threshold of the new.

Looking backward

CHRISTINA ROSSETTI

1830–1894

From
Songs for Strangers and Pilgrims

Looking back along life's trodden way,
    Gleams and greenness linger on the track:
Distance melts and mellows all today,
    Looking back.

Rose and purple and a silvery grey,
    Is that cloud the cloud we called so black?
Evening harmonises all today,
    Looking back.

Foolish feet so prone to halt or stray,
    Foolish heart so restive on the rack!
Yesterday we sighed, but not today,
    Looking back.

KATHLEEN RAINE

1908–

A Nice Little World

My mother, nearing her end of days
Said, in retrospective gratitude,
She being elsewhere bound,
'But this is a nice little world.'
I too have found
Shelter here, birds, stars, waters, flowers, trees,
Kindness, dear human faces,
I too, *ils m'effroyent*, the eternal spaces.

161

E. NESBIT

1858–1924

The Things that Matter

Now that I've nearly done my days,
    And grown too stiff to sweep or sew,
I sit and think till I'm amaze
    About what lots of things I know:
Things as I've found out one by one –
    And when I'm fast down in the clay,
My knowing things and how they're done
    Will all be lost and thrown away.

There's things I know as won't be lost,
    Things as folk write and talk about:
The way to keep your roots from frost,
    And how to get your ink spots out.
What medicine's good for sores and sprains,
    What way to salt your butter down,
What charms will cure your different pains,
    And what will bright your faded gown.

But more important things than these,
    They can't be written in a book:
How fast to boil your greens and peas,
    And how good bacon ought to look;
The feel of real good wearing stuff,
    The kind of apple as will keep,
The look of bread that's rose enough,
    And how to get a child asleep.

Whether the jam is fit to pot,
    Whether the milk is going to turn,
Whether a hen will lay or not,
    Is things as some folks never learn.
I know the weather by the sky,
    I know what herbs grow in what lane;
And if sick men are going to die,
    Or if they'll get about again.

162

Young wives come in, a-smiling, grave,
   With secrets that they itch to tell:
I know what sort of times they'll have,
   And if they'll have a boy or gell.
And if a lad is ill to bind,
   Or some young maid is hard to lead,
I know when you should speak 'em kind,
   And when it's scolding as they need.

I used to know where birds ud set,
   And likely spots for trout or hare,
And God may want me to forget
   The way to set a line or snare;
But not the way to truss a chick,
   To fry a fish or baste a roast,
Nor how to tell, when folk are sick,
   What kind of herb will ease them most!

Forgetting seems such silly waste!
   I know so many little things,
And now the Angels will make haste
   To dust it all away with wings!
O God, you made me like to know,
   You kept the things straight in my head,
Please God, if you can make it so,
   Let me know *something* when I'm dead.

WALTER DE LA MARE

1873–1956

Alone

A very old woman
Lives in yon house.
The squeak of the cricket,
The stir of the mouse,
Are all she knows
Of the earth and us.

Once she was young,
Would dance and play,
Like many another
Young popinjay;
And run to her mother
At dusk of day.

And colours bright
She delighted in;
The fiddle to hear,
And to lift her chin,
And sing as small
As a twittering wren.

But age apace
Comes at last to all;
And a lone house filled
With the cricket's call;
And the scampering mouse
In the hollow wall.

JENNY JOSEPH

1932–

Trompe l'Oeil

(A visit to an old woman sitting at home)

Old woman
Sitting by the fire
Making a lap from spread legs, and the scarfed outline
Of the little old body in the picture books;
Veined hand forcefully on knee to heave you up
From mental dawdlings mulling by the fire
In order to fetch something, to laugh, to make a rough crack,
Tough enough as old boots are to be capacious
For the lumpy foot that can fit none of the shoes
On offer in the shops; —

Stop being busy and practical for a minute,
Turn your head.
I've blown the cover you use for every day.
You can bring out now the small child from the folds
Of the air where you've hidden her about your person.
She is rising through the palimpsest
Of the way you lean and look and scramble up,
As a shadow strengthens at the strengthening sun.
There's still this young fruit, this kernel, this shape in little
From which the tree has grown,
Not child of your womb, or child's child that, separating,
Continued your life elsewhere, but – ghost if you like,
Pattern within the substance, – rings of a tree
Still living in the wood for the eightieth year
To be there too.

You have withdrawn to look for something to show me
Leaving me in the company of a small bright child
Sitting by the fire heaving its cat in its arms.

MARGARET CROPPER

1886–1980

Growing Old

You need to be humble when you're growing old
You need to look at what the spring is doing
Putting forth little treasures, primroses and the like,
You need to be faithful when you're growing old
You must take care of all that life has given,
And keep it gratefully, for these quiet days –
Full of thanksgiving for the beauty you've seen,
In people, and growing life and quiet skies –
Old age is full of last chances – words to a friend
A quiet love, hands that are still held out
For a loving clasp that tells of long love.

WILLIAM SHAKESPEARE

1564–1616

From *King Henry the Fifth, Act IV Scene 3*

He that shall live this day, and see old age,
Will yearly on the vigil feast his neighbours,
And say, to-morrow is Saint Crispian
Then will he strip his sleeve and shew his scars:
And say 'these wounds I had on Crispin's day'
Old men forget; yet all shall be forgot,
But he'll remember, with advantages
What feats he did that day: Then shall our names,
Familiar in his mouth as household words,
Harry the king, Bedford and Exeter,
Warwick and Talbot, Salisbury and Gloucester,
Be in their flowing cups freshly remember'd:
This story shall the good man teach his son;
And Crispin Crispian shall n'er go by,
From this day to the ending of the world,
But we in it shall be remembered;
We few, we happy few, we band of brothers.

GEORGE PEELE

1558?–1597

A Farewell to Arms
(To Queen Elizabeth)

His golden locks Time hath to silver turn'd;
  O Time too swift, O swiftness never ceasing!
His youth 'gainst time and age hath ever spurn'd,
  But spurn'd in vain; youth waneth by increasing:
Beauty, strength, youth, are flowers but fading seen;
Duty, faith, love, are roots, and ever green.

His helmet now shall make a hive for bees;
   And, lovers' sonnets turn'd to holy psalms,
A man-at-arms must now serve on his knees,
   And feed on prayers, which are Age his alms:
But though from court to cottage he depart,
His Saint is sure of his unspotted heart.

And when he saddest sits in homely cell,
   He'll teach his swains this carol for a song, –
'Blest be the hearts that wish my sovereign well
   Curst be the souls that think her any wrong,'
Goddess, allow this aged man his right
To be your beadsman now that was your knight.

W.B. YEATS

1865–1939

The Lamentation of the Old Pensioner

Although I shelter from the rain
Under a broken tree,
My chair was nearest to the fire
In every company
That talked of love or politics,
Ere Time transfigured me.

Though lads are making pikes again
For some conspiracy,
And crazy rascals rage their fill
At human tyranny;
My contemplations are of Time
That has transfigured me.

There's not a woman turns her face
Upon a broken tree,
And yet the beauties that I loved
Are in my memory;
I spit into the face of Time
That has transfigured me.

EDITH SITWELL

1887–1964

An Old Woman Laments in Spring-time

I walk on grass as soft as wool,
Or fluff that our old fingers pull
From beaver or from miniver, –
Sweet-sounding as a dulcimer, –

A poor old woman creeping where
The young can never pry and stare.
I am so old, I should be gone, –
Too old to warm in the kind sun

My wrinkled face; my hat that flaps
Will hide it, and may coat has laps
The trail upon the grass as I
Like some warm shade of spring creep by.

And all the laden fruit-boughs spread
Into a silver sound, but dead
Is the wild dew I used to know,
Nor will the morning music grow.

I sit beneath these coral boughs
Where the air's silver plumage grows
And flows like water with a sigh.
Fed with sweet milk of lilies, I

Still feel the dew like amber gums,
That from the richest spice-tree comes,
Drip down upon my turbanned head,
Trembling and ancient as the Dead,

Beneath these floating branches' shade.
Yet long ago, a lovely maid,

168

On grass, a fading silver tune
Played on an ancient dulcimer,
(And soft as wool of miniver)

I walked like a young antelope,
And Day was but an Ethiop,
Beside my fairness shining there –
Like black shade seemed the brightest air

When I was lovely as the snows, –
A fading starriness that flows –
Then far-off Death seemed but the shade
That those heavenly branches made.

ALFRED, LORD TENNYSON

1809–1892

In the Valley of Cauteretz

All along the valley, stream that flashest white,
Deepening thy voice with the deepening of the night,
All along the valley, where thy waters flow,
I walked with one I loved two and thirty years ago.
All along the valley, where I walked today,
The two and thiry years were a mist that rolls away:
For all along the valley, down thy rocky bed,
Thy living voice to me was as the voice of the dead,
And all along the valley, by rock and cave and tree,
The voice of the dead was a living voice to me.

KATHLEEN RAINE

1908–

Christmas-Tree

For whom have I
As yet another year is ending

Decked this Christmas-tree
In blown-glass coloured balls and birds and shining spheres
And glitter on the ever-green
And living boughs? Who of the young
Who will come briefly to visit me
Will find magic in these tinsel stars, hear what they sing
Of memories not theirs, who must live on
Into years farther yet from Bethlehem?
No, not for the living,
It is my ghosts who will keep Christmas Past with me,
As it should be that an old woman
In all my remembered and unremembered presents be
With those who loved me, yet with whom, indifferent then,
Only now I am.

R.S. THOMAS

1913–

The Country Clergy

I see them working in old rectories
By the sun's light, by candlelight,
Venerable men, their black cloth
A little dusty, a little green
With holy mildew. And yet their skulls,
Ripening over so many prayers,
Toppled into the same grave
With oafs and yokels. They left no books,
Memorial to their lonely thought
In grey parishes; rather they wrote
On men's hearts and in the minds
Of young children sublime words
Too soon forgotten. God in his time
Or out of time will correct this.

PHILIP LARKIN

1922–1985

Continuing to Live

Continuing to live – that is, repeat
A habit formed to get necessaries –
Is nearly always losing, or going without.
  It varies.

This loss of interest, hair, and enterprise –
Ah, if the game were poker, yes,
You might discard them, draw a full house!
  But it's chess.

And once you have walked the length of your mind, what
You command is as clear as a lading-list.
Anything else must not, for you, be thought
  To exist.

And what's the profit? Only that, in time,
We half-identify the blind impress
All our behavings bear, may trace it home.
  But to confess.

On that green evening when our death begins,
Just what it was, is hardly satisfying,
Since it applied only to one man once,
  And that one dying.

THOMAS MOORE

1779–1852

The Light of Other Days

Oft in the stilly night,
  Ere slumber's chain has bound me,

171

Fond Memory brings the light
  Of other days around me:
    The smiles, the tears
    Of boyhood's years,
  The word of love then spoken;
    The eyes that shone,
    Now dimm'd and gone,
  The cheerful hearts now broken!
Thus in the stilly night,
  Ere slumber's chain has bound me,
Sad Memory brings the light
  Of other days around me.

When I remember all
  The friends, so link'd together,
I've seen them round me fall
  Like leaves in wintry weather,
    I feel like one
    Who treads alone
  Some banquet-hall deserted,
    Whose lights are fled
    Whose garlands dead,
  And all but he departed!
Thus in the stilly night,
  Ere slumber's chain has bound me,
Sad Memory brings the light
  Of other days around me.

ROBERT BRIDGES

1844–1930

Winter Nightfall

The day begins to droop, –
  Its course is done:
But nothing tells the place
  Of the setting sun.

The hazy darkness deepens,
 And up the lane
You may hear, but cannot see,
 The homing wain.

An engine pants and hums
 In the farm hard by;
Its lowering smoke is lost
 In the lowering sky.

The soaking branches drip,
 And all night through
The dropping will not cease
 In the avenue.

A tall man there in the house
 Must keep his chair:
He knows he will never again
 Breathe the spring air:

His heart is worn with work;
 He is giddy and sick
If he rise to go as far
 As the nearest rick:

He thinks of his morn of life,
 His hale, strong years;
And braves as he may the night
 Of darkness and tears.

ROBERT BRIDGES

1844–1930

Fortunate Nimium

I have lain in the sun
I have toil'd as I might
I have thought as I would
And now it is night.

My bed full of sleep
My heart of content
For friends that I met
The way that I went.

I welcome fatigue
While frenzy and care
Like thin summer clouds
Go melting in air.

To dream as I may
And awake when I will
With the song of the birds
And the sun on the hill.

Or death – were it death –
To what should I wake
Who loved in my home
All life for its sake?

What good have I wrought?
I laugh to have learned
That joy cannot come
Unless it be earned;

For a happier lot
Than God giveth me
It never hath been
Nor ever shall be.

W.B. YEATS

1865–1939

Youth and Age

Much did I rage when young,
Being by the world oppressed.
But now with flattering tongue
It speeds the parting guest.

EUGENE LEE-HAMILTON

1845–1907

Lost Years

My boyhood went: it went where went the trace
Left by the pony's hoofs upon the sand;
It went where went the stream sought rod in hand;
It went where went the ice on the pond's face.
Then went my youth: it went where Dawn doth chase
The ballroom's lights aways with pearly wand;
It went where went the echoes of the band;
It went where go the nights that steal Day's place.

And now my manhood goes where goes the song
Of captive birds, the cry of crippled things;
It goes where goes the day that unused dies.
The cage is narrow and the bars are strong
In which my restless spirit beats its wings;
And round me stretch unfathomable skies.

W.B. YEATS

1865–1939

The Old Men Admiring themselves
in the Water

I heard the old, old men say,
'Everything alters,
And one by one we drop away,'
They had hands like claws, and their knees
Were twisted like the old thorn-trees
By the waters.
I heard the old, old men say,
'All that is beautiful drifts away
Like the waters'.

175

WALTER SAVAGE LANDOR

1775–1864

Late Leaves

The leaves are falling; so am I;
    The few late leaves have moisture in the eye;
        So have I too.
Scarcely on any bough is heard
Joyous, or even unjoyous bird
        The whole wood through.

Winter may come; he brings but nigher
    His circle (yearly narrowing) to the fire
        Where old friends meet.
Let him; now heaven is overcast,
And spring and summer both are past,
        And all things sweet.

ANDREW YOUNG

1885–1971

The Old Man

I listened to the grasshoppers
    Like small machines mowing the hay,
Hot and content to think myself
    As busy and idle as they.

A woman sat under a tree
    Cursing the flies that tormented her;
I did not stop with 'Which is the way
    By Herbert's Hole to Ballinger?'

I thought of that old man I asked
    Who saw each meadow, stile and lane

176

Clear as pebbles washed by the Chess
And never shall see them again.

G.K. CHESTERTON

1874–1936

Gold Leaves

Lo! I am come to autumn,
 When all the leaves are gold;
Grey hairs and golden leaves cry out
 The year and I are old.

In youth I sought the prince of men,
 Captain in cosmic wars,
Our Titan, even the weeds would show
 Defiant to the stars.

But now a great thing in the street
 Seems any human nod,
Where shift in strange democracy
 The million masks of God.

In youth I sought the golden flower
 Hidden in wood or wold,
But I am come to autumn,
 When all the leaves are gold.

P.R. HIGGINS

1896–1942

The Old Jockey

His last days linger in that low attic
That barely lets out the night,
With its gabled window on Knackers' Alley,
Just hoodwinking the light.

He comes and goes by that gabled window
And then on the window-pane
He leans, as thin as a bottled shadow –
A look and he's gone again:

Eyeing, maybe, some fine fish-women
In the best shawls of the Coombe,
Or, maybe, the knife-grinder plying his treadle,
A run of sparks from this thumb!

But, O you should see him gazing, gazing,
When solemnly out on the road
The horse-drays pass overladen with grasses,
Each driver lost in his load;

Gazing until they return; and suddenly,
As galloping by they race,
From his pale eyes, like glass breaking,
Light leaps on his face.

GEORGE GASCOIGNE

c. 1534–1577

A Lullaby

Sing lullaby, as women do,
   Wherewith they bring their babes to rest;
And lullaby can I sing too,
   As womanly as can the best.
With lullaby they still the child;
And if I be not much beguiled,
Full many a wanton babe have I,
Which must be still'd with lullaby.

First lullaby my youthful years,
   It is now time to go to bed:
For crooked age and hoary hairs
   Have won the haven within my head.

With lullaby then, youth be still;
With lullaby content thy will;
Since courage quails and comes behind,
Go sleep, and so beguile thy mind!

Next lullaby my gazing eyes,
   Which wonted were to glance apace;
For every glass may now suffice
   To show the furrows in thy face.
With lullaby then wink awhile;
With lullaby your looks beguile;
Let no fair face, nor beauty bright,
Entice you eft with vain delight.

And lullaby my wanton will;
   Let reason's rule now reign thy thought;
Since all too late I find by skill
   How dear I have thy fancies bought:
With lullaby now take thine ease,
With lullaby thy doubts appease;
For trust to this, if thou be still,
My body shall obey thy will.

Thus lullaby my youth, mine eyes,
   My will, my ware, and all that was:
I can no more delays devise;
   But welcome pain, let pleasures pass.
With lullaby now take your leave;
With lullaby your dreams deceive;
And when you rise with waking eye,
Remember then this lullaby.

SAMUEL TAYLOR COLERIDGE

1772–1834

Youth and Age

Verse, a breeze 'mid blossoms straying,
Where Hope clung feeding, like a bee –

Both were mine! Life went a-maying
With Nature, Hope and Poesy,
      When I was young!
When I was young? – Ah, woeful When!
Ah! for the change 'twixt Now and Then!
This breathing house not built with hands,
This body that does me grievous wrong,
O'er aery cliffs and glittering sands,
How lightly then it flash'd along –
Like those trim skiffs, unkown of yore,
On winding lakes and rivers wide,
That ask no aid of sail or oar,
That fear no spite of wind or tide!
Naught cared this body for wind or weather
When Youth and I lived in't together.

Flowers are lovely! Love is flower-like;
Friendship is a sheltering tree;
O the joys, that came down shower-like,
Of Friendship, Love, and Liberty,
      Ere I was old!
Ere I was old? Ah, woeful Ere,
Which tells me, Youth's no longer here!
O Youth! for years so many and sweet,
'Tis known that thou and I were one;
I'll think it but a fond conceit –
It cannot be that thou art gone!
Thy vesper-bell hath not yet toll'd –
And thou wert aye a masker bold!
What strange disguise hast now put on,
To make believe that thou art gone?
I see these locks in silvery slips,
This drooping gait, this altered size;
But springtime blossoms on thy lips,
And tears take sunshine from thine eyes!
Life is but thought; so think I will
That Youth and I are housemates still.

Dewdrops are the gems of morning,
But the tears of mournful eve!
Where no hope is, life's a warning
That only serves to make us grieve,
      When we are old!
With oft and tedious taking-leave,
Like some poor nigh-related guest
That may not rudely be dismist,
Yet hath outstayed his welcome while,
And tells the jest without the smile.

CHARLOTTE MEW

1869–1928

Old Shepherd's Prayer

Up to the bed by the window, where I be lyin',
Comes bells and bleat of the flock wi' they two children's
                   clack.
Over, from under the eaves there's the starlings flyin',
And down in yard, fit to burst his chain, yapping out at
                Sue I do hear young Mac.

Turning around like a falled-over sack
I can see team ploughin' in Whithy-bush field and meal carts
             startin' up road to Church-Town;
Saturday arternoon the men goin' back
And the women from market, trapin' home over the down.

Heavenly Master, I wud like to wake to they same green places
Where I be know'd for breakin' dogs and follerin' sheep,
And if I may not walk in th' old ways and look on th' old
                    faces
I wud sooner sleep.

THOMAS HARDY

1840–1928

He never expected much,
or a Consideration on my
Eighty-sixth Birthday

Well, World, you have kept faith with me,
    Kept faith with me;
Upon the whole you have proved to be
    Much as you said you were.
Since as a child I used to lie
Upon the leaze and watch the sky,
Never, I own, expected I
    That life would be all fair.

'Twas then you said, and since have said,
    Times since have said,
In that mysterious voice you shed
    From clouds and hills around:
'Many have loved me desperately,
Many with smooth serenity,
While some have shown contempt of me
    Till they dropped underground.

'I do not promise overmuch,
    Child, overmuch;
Just neutral-tinted haps and such,'
    You said to minds like mine.
Wise warning for your credit's sake!
Which I for one failed not to take,
And hence could stem such strain and ache
    As each year might assign.

JOHN MEADE FALKNER

1858–1932

Christmas Day: The Family Sitting

In the days of Caesar Augustus
   There went forth this decree:
Si quis rectus et justus
   Liveth in Galilee
Let him go up to Jerusalem
   And pay his scot to me.

There are passed after another
   Christmases fifty-three,
Since I sat here with my mother
   And heard the great decree:
How they went up to Jerusalem
   Out of Galilee.

They have passed one after another;
   Father and Mother died,
Brother and sister and brother,
   Taken and sanctified.
I am left alone in the sitting,
   With none to sit beside.

On the flyleaves of these old prayer-books
   The childish writings fade,
Which show that once they were their books
   In the days when prayer was made
For other kings and princesses,
   William and Adelaide.

The pillars are twisted with holly,
   And the font is wreathed with yew.
Christ forgive me for folly,
   Youth's lapses – not a few,
For the hardness of my middle life,
   For age's fretful view.

Cotton-wool letters on scarlet,
 All the ancient lore,
Tell how the chieftains starlit
 Came to Bethlehem to adore;
To hail Him King in the manger,
 Wonderful, Counsellor.

The bells ring out in the steeple
 The gladness of erstwhile,
And the children of other people
 Are walking up the aisle;
They brush my elbow in passing,
 Some turn to give me a smile.

Is the almond-blossom bitter?
 Is the grasshopper heavy to bear?
Christ make me happier, fitter
 To go to my own over there;
Jerusalem the Golden,
 What bliss beyond compare!

My Lord, where I have offended
 Do Thou forgive it me
That so, when all being ended,
 I hear Thy last decree
I may go up to Jerusalem
 Out of Galilee.

WALTER SAVAGE LANDOR

1775–1864

Finis

I strove with none, for none was worth my strife.
Nature I loved, and next to Nature, Art;
I warm'd both hands before the fire of life;
It sinks, and I am ready to depart.

Looking forward

CHRISTINA ROSSETTI

1830–1894

Passing Away

Passing away, saith the World, passing away:
Chances, beauty and youth, sapped day by day:
Thy life never continueth in one stay.
Is the eye waxen dim, is the dark hair changing to grey
That hath won neither laurel nor bay?
I shall clothe myself in Spring and bud in May,
Thou, root-stricken, shall not rebuild thy decay
On my bosom for aye.
Then I answered: Yea.

Passing away, saith my Soul, passing away:
With its burden of fear and hope, of labour and play,
Hearken what the past doth witness and say:
Rust in thy gold, a moth is in thine array,
A canker is in thy bud, thy leaf must decay.
At midnight, at cockcrow, at morning, one certain day
Lo the Bridegroom shall come and shall not delay;
Watch thou and pray.
Then I answered: Yea.

Passing away, saith my God, passing away:
Winter passeth after the long delay:
New grapes on the vine, new figs on the tender spray,
Turtle calleth turtle in Heaven's May.
Though I tarry, wait for Me, trust Me, watch and pray:
Arise, come away, night is past and lo it is day,
My love, My sister, My spouse, thou shalt hear Me say.
Then I answered: Yea.

WALTER DE LA MARE
1873–1956

Dust to Dust

Heavenly Archer, bend thy bow;
Now the flame of life burns low,
Youth is gone; I too would go.

Ever Fortune leads to this:
Harsh or kind, at last she is
Murderess of all ecstasies.

Yet the spirit, dark, alone,
Bound in sense, still hearkens on
For tidings of a bliss foregone.

Sleep is well for dreamless head,
At no breath astonished,
From the Gardens of the Dead.

I the immortal harps hear ring,
By Babylon's river languishing.
Heavenly Archer, loose thy string.

CATHERINE CARSWELL
1879–1946

Envoy

It will not be long now, my soul,
Not long.
Till that comes that filled you with fears
These many years,
But now not at all.

I have had children, I have had lovers
I feared to leave.
Now I am alone. I have put all from me,
And have ceased to grieve.

Once, long ago, I was alone,
Before life took me and played with my heart.
Now again, my solitary fountain
Rises apart.

In joy it rises
From a deeper source than before,
Joy to have lived, and this deeper joy
Soon to live no more.

CAROLINE SOUTHEY

1787–1854

To Death

Come not in terrors clad, to claim
   An unresisting prey:
Come like an evening shadow, Death!
   So stealthily, so silently!
And shut my eyes, and steal my breath;
   Then willingly, O willingly,
     With thee I'll go away!

What need to clutch with iron grasp
   What gentlest touch may take?
What need with aspect dark to scare
   So awfully, so terribly,
The weary soul would hardly care,
   Call'd quietly, call'd tenderly,
     From thy dread power to break?

'Tis not as when thou markest out
   The young, the blest, the gay,
The loved, the loving – they who dream
   So happily, so hopefully;
Then harsh thy kindest call may seem
   And shrinkingly, reluctantly,
     The summon'd may obey.

But I have drunk enough of life –
   The cup assigned to me
Dash'd with a little sweet at best,
   So scantily, so scantily –
To know full well that all the rest
   More bitterly, more bitterly,
     Drugged to the last will be.

And I may live to pain some heart
   That kindly cares for me:
To pain, but not to bless. O Death!
   Come quietly – come lovingly –
And shut mine eyes, and steal my breath;
   Then willingly, O willingly,
     I'll go away with thee!

CAROLINA LADY NAIRNE

1766–1845

The Land o' the Leal

I'm wearin' awa', John
Like snaw-wreaths in thaw, John,
I'm wearin' awa'
   To the land o' the leal.
There's nae sorrow there, John,
There's neither cauld nor care, John,
The day is aye fair
   In the land o' the leal.

Our bonnie bairn's there, John,
She was baith gude and fair, John;
And O! we grudged her sair
   To the land o' the leal.
But sorrow's sel' wears past, John,
And joy's a-coming fast, John,
The joy that's aye to last
   In the land o' the leal.

Sae dear the joy was bought, John,
Sae free the battle fought, John,
That sinfu' man e'er bought
   To the land o' the leal.
O, dry your glistening e'e, John!
My soul langs to be free, John,
And angels beckon me
    To the land o' the leal.

O, haud ye leal and true, John!
Your day it's wearin' through, John,
And I'll welcome you
   To the land o' the leal.
Now fare-ye-weel, my ain John,
This warld's cares are vain, John,
We'll meet, and we'll be fain,
   In the land o' the leal.

WILLIAM SAVAGE LANDOR

1775–1864

Years

Years, many parti-coloured years,
Some have crept on, and some have flown
Since first before me fell those tears
I never could see fall alone.

Years, not so many, are to come,
Years not so varied, when from you
One more will fall; when carried home,
I see it not, nor hear *Adieu*.

FRANCES CORNFORD

1886–1960

The Old Men outside an Inn

Somewhere their shoulders have begun to bow
As if in deference to earth, who now
May any day invite them to be done
Quite quietly with bench and beer and sun.

WALTER DE LA MARE

1873–1956

The Old Men

Old and alone, sit we,
　　Caged, riddle-rid men;
Lost to Earth's 'Listen!' and 'See!'
　　Thought's 'Wherefore?' and 'When?'

Only far memories stray
　　Of a past once lovely, but now
Wasted and faded away,
　　Like green leaves from the bough.

Vast broods the silence of night,
　　The ruinous moon
Lifts on our faces her light,
　　Whence all dreaming is gone.

We speak not; trembles each head;
    In their sockets our eyes are still;
Desire as cold as the dead;
    Without wonder or will.

And One, with a lanthorn, draws near,
    At clash with the moon in our eyes;
'Where are thou?' he asks: 'I am here',
    One by one we arise.

And none lifts a hand to withhold
    A friend from the touch of that foe;
Heart cried unto heart 'Thou are old!'
    Yet, reluctant, we go.

ROBERT BROWNING

1812–1889

Prospice

Fear death? – to feel the fog in my throat,
    The mist in my face,
When the snows begin, and the blasts denote
    I am nearing the place,
The power of the night, the press of the storm,
    The post of the foe;
Where he stands, the Arch Fear in a visible form,
    Yet the strong man must go:
For the journey is done and the summit attained,
    And the barriers fall,
Though a battle's to fight ere the guerdon be gained,
    The reward of it all.
I was ever a fighter, so – one fight more,
    The best and the last!
I would hate that death bandaged my eyes, and forbore,
    And bade me creep past.
No! let me taste the whole of it, fare like my peers
    The heroes of old,

Bear the brunt, in a minute pay glad life's arrears
    Of pain, darkness and cold.
For sudden the worst turns the best to the brave,
    The black minute's at end,
And the elements' rage, the fiend-voices that rave,
    Shall dwindle, shall blend,
Shall change, shall become first a peace out of pain,
    Then a light, then thy breast,
O thou soul of my soul! I shall clasp thee again,
    And with God be the rest!

DIANA HENDRY

1941–

Prayer for Rain

Lord, you who can make
The Australian desert flower
with a single rainfall
once in seventy years

remember me, whose
three score years and ten
are running out.

From *The Spectator*, 19 May 1990

WILLIAM WORDSWORTH

1770–1850

From *The Primrose of the Rock*

Sin-blighted though we are, we too
    The reasoning Sons of Men,
From one oblivious winter called
    Shall rise, and breathe again;
And in eternal summer lose
    Our threescore years and ten.

To humbleness of heart descends
   This prescience from on high,
The faith that elevates the just,
   Before and when they die;
And makes each soul a separate heaven,
   A court for Deity.

RICHARD GARNETT

1835–1906

Sonnet – Age

I will not rail or grieve when torpid eld
Frosts the slow-journeying blood, for I shall see
The lovelier leaves hang yellow on the tree,
The nimbler brooks in icy fetters held.
Methinks the aged eye that first beheld
Pale Autumn in her waning pageantry,
Then knew himself, dear Nature, child of thee,
Marking the common doom, that all compelled.

No kindred we to her beloved broods,
If, dying these, we draw a selfish breath;
But one path travel all her multitudes,
And none dispute the solemn Voice that saith:
Sun to thy setting; to your autumn, woods;
Stream to thy sea; and man unto thy death.

STEPHEN HAWES

c. 1475–1511

His Epitaph

O mortal folk, you may behold and see
   How I lie here, sometime a mighty knight.

The end of joy and all prosperity
    Is death at last. thorough his course and might;
    After the day there cometh the dark night,
      For though the day be never so long,
      At last the bells ringeth to evensong.

OLIVER GOGARTY

1878–1957

Non Dolet

Our friends go with us as we go
Down the long path where Beauty wends,
Where all we love forgathers, so
Why should we fear to join our friends?

Who would survive them to outlast
His children; to outwear his fame —
Left when the Triumph has gone past —
To win from Age not Time a name?

Then do not shudder at the Knife
That Death's indifferent hand drives home;
But with the Strivers leave the strife,
Nor, after Caesar, skulk in Rome.

RODEN NOEL

1834–1894

The Old

They are waiting on the shore
    For the bark to take them home:
They will toil and grieve no more;
    The hour for release has come.

All their long life lies behind
 Like a dimly blending dream:
Therein nothing left to bind
 To the realms that only seem.

They are waiting for the boat;
 There is nothing left to do:
What was near them grows remote,
 Happy silence falls like dew;
Now the shadowy bark is come,
And the weary may go home.

By still water they would rest
 In the shadow of the tree.
After battle sleep is best,
 After noise, tranquility.

WILLIAM ERNEST HENLEY

1849–1903

Margaritae Sorori

A late lark twitters from the quiet skies,
And from the west,
Where the sun, his day's work ended,
Lingers as in content,
There falls on the old, gray city
An influence luminous and serene,
A shining peace.

The smoke ascends
In a rosy-and-golden haze. The spires
Shine and are changed. In the valley
Shadows rise. The lark sings on. The sun,
Closing his benediction,
Sinks, and the darkening air
Thrills with a sense of the triumphing night —
Night with her gift of stars
And her great gift of sleep.

So be my passing!
My task accomplished and the long day done,
My wages taken, and in my heart
Some late lark singing,
Let me gathered to the quiet west,
The sundown splendid and serene,
Death.

ANNA LAETITIA BARBAULD

1743–1824

From *Life*

Life! we have been long together,
Through pleasant and through cloudy weather;
  'Tis hard to part when friends are dear;
  Perhaps 'twill cost a sigh, a tear; —
  Then steal away, give little warning,
   Choose thine own time;
Say not Good-night, but in some brighter clime
   Bid me Good-morning!

ALFRED, LORD TENNYSON

1809–1892

Crossing the Bar

Sunset and evening star,
 And one clear call for me!
And may there be no moaning of the bar,
 When I put out to sea

But such a tide as moving seems asleep,
 Too full for sound and foam,
When that which drew from out the boundless deep
 Turns again home.

Twilight and evening bell,
 And after that the dark!
And may there be no sadness of farewell,
 When I embark;

For tho' from out our bourne of Time and Place
 The flood may bear me far,
I hope to see my Pilot face to face
 When I have crost the bar.

T.S. ELIOT

1888–1965

A Song for Simeon

Lord, the Roman hyacinths are blooming in bowls and
The winter sun creeps by the snow hills;
The stubborn season has made stand.
My life is light, waiting for the death wind,
Like a feather on the back of my hand.
Dust in sunlight and memory in corners
Wait for the wind that chills towards the dead land.

Grant us thy peace.
I have walked many years in this city,
Kept faith and fast, provided for the poor,
Have given and taken honour and ease.
There was never any rejected from my door.
Who shall remember my house, where shall live my children's
children
When the time of sorrow is come?
They will take to the goat's path, and the fox's home,
Fleeing from foreign faces and the foreign swords.

Before the time of cords and scourges and lamentation
Grant us thy peace.

Before the stations of the mountain of desolation,
Before the certain hour of maternal sorrow,
Now at this birth season of decease,
Let the Infant, the still unspeaking and unspoken Word,
Grand Israel's consolation
To one who has eighty years and no tomorrow.

According to thy word.
They shall praise thee and suffer in every generation
With glory and derision,
Light upon light, mounting the saints' stair.
Not for me the martyrdom, the ecstasy of thought and prayer,
Not for me the ultimate vision.
Grant me thy peace.
(And a sword shall pierce thy heart,
Thine also).
I am tired with my own life and the lives of those after me,
I am dying in my own death and the deaths of those after me,
Let thy servant depart,
Having seen thy salvation.

THOMAS CAMPION

1567?–1619

O Come Quickly!

Never weather-beaten sail more willing bent to shore,
Never tired pilgrim's limbs affected slumber more,
Then my wearied sprite now longs to fly out of my troubled breast;
O come quickly, sweetest Lord, and take my soul to rest!

Ever blooming are the joys of heaven's high Paradise,
Cold age deafs not there our ears nor vapour dims our eyes;
Glory there the sun outshines; whose beams the Blessed only see:
O come quickly, glorious Lord, and raise my sprite to Thee!

WILLIAM WORDSWORTH

1770–1850

Afterthought

(Last sonnet in the River Duddon sequence)

I thought of Thee, my partner and my guide,
As being past away – Vain sympathies!
For, backward, Duddon! as I cast my eyes,
I see what was, and is, and will abide;
Still glides the Stream, and shall for ever glide;
The Form remains, the Function never dies;
While we, the brave, the mighty, and the wise,
We Men, who in our morn of youth defied
The elements, must vanish; – be it so!
Enough, if something from our hands have power
To live, and act, and serve the future hour;
And if, as toward the silent tomb we go,
Through love, through hope, and faith's transcendent dower,
We feel that we are greater than we know.

Epilogue

WALTER SAVAGE LANDOR

1775–1864

On His own Death

Death stands above me, whispering low
   I know not what into my ear:
Of his strange language all I know
   Is, there is not a word of fear.

Index of authors

Index of first lines